Angels, Fairies, Demons, and the Elementals

Angels, Fairies, Demons, and the Elementals

*With an Edgar Cayce Perspective
on the Supernatural World*

JOHN VAN AUKEN

A.R.E. Press   •   Virginia Beach   •   Virginia

A.R.E. Press
215 67th Street
Virginia Beach, VA 23451-2061

ISBN 13: 978-0-87604-770-5

Cover design by Christine Fulcher

Contents

Illustrations

About Edgar Cayce

dgar Cayce (pronounced *KAY-see*, the same as the English name *Casey*) was born on a farm near Hopkinsville, Kentucky, on March 18, 1877. As a child, he displayed unusual powers of perception. At the age of six, he told his parents that he could see and talk with "visions," sometimes of relatives who had recently died, and on occasion he saw angels. He could also sleep with his head on his schoolbooks and awaken with a photographic recall of their contents, even citing the page number upon which the answer appeared. However, after completing seventh grade, he left school—which was not unusual for boys of his age at that time.

When he was twenty-one, he developed a paralysis of the throat muscles that caused him to lose his voice. When doctors were unable to find a physical cause for this condition, Edgar Cayce asked an acquaintance to help him re-enter the same kind of hypnotic sleep that had enabled him to memorize his schoolbooks as a child. The friend gave him the necessary suggestions, and once he was in this trance-like state,

Cayce spoke clearly and directly without any difficulty. He instructed the "hypnotist" to give him a suggestion to increase the blood flow to his throat; when the suggestion was given, Cayce's throat turned blood red. Then, while still under hypnosis, Cayce recommended some specific medication and manipulative therapy that would aid in restoring his voice completely.

On subsequent occasions, Cayce would go into the hypnotic state to diagnose bodily conditions and prescribe a course of action to restore health. Doctors around Hopkinsville and Bowling Green, Kentucky, took advantage of Cayce's unique talent to diagnose their patients. They soon discovered that all Cayce needed was the name and address of a patient to "tune in" telepathically to that individual's mind and body. The patients didn't have to be near Cayce, he could tune-in to them wherever they were.

When one of the young MDs working with Cayce submitted a report on his strange abilities to a clinical research society in Boston, the reactions were ones of astonishment. On October 9, 1910, *The New York Times* carried two pages of headlines and pictures. From then on, people from all over the country sought the so-called "Sleeping Prophet," a nickname that came from one of the many books written about him.

The routine he used for conducting a trance-diagnosis was to recline on a couch with his hands over his "third eye" region on his forehead. When he saw a white light, he moved his hands to his solar-plexus. At this time, his eyelids would begin fluttering, and his breathing would become deep and rhythmic. This was the signal to the conductor (usually his wife, Gertrude) to make verbal contact with Cayce's sub-conscious by giving a suggestion. Unless this procedure was timed to synchronize with his fluttering eyelids and the change in his breathing, Cayce would proceed beyond his trance state and simply fall fast asleep. However, once the suggestion was made, Cayce would access whatever or whoever was necessary to fulfill the suggestion. In his health cases, he would proceed to describe the patient as though he or she were sitting right next to him, and his mind was functioning much as an x-ray scanner, seeing into every organ of the inquirer's body. When he was finished, he would say, "Ready for questions." However, in many cases, his mind would have already anticipated the patient's questions, answering them during the main session. Eventually, he would say, "We are through for the present," whereupon the conductor would give the suggestion for him to return to normal consciousness and balance the energies in his body.

If this procedure were in any way violated, Cayce would be in serious personal danger. On one occasion, he remained in a trance state for three days and had actually been given up for dead by the attending doctors.

At each session, a stenographer (usually Gladys Davis, his personal secretary) would record in shorthand everything Cayce said. Sometimes, during a trance session, Cayce would even correct the stenographer's spelling. It was as though his mind were in touch with everything around him and beyond.

Each client was identified with a number in an effort to keep their names private. For example, hypnotic material for Edgar Cayce is filed under the number 294. His first "reading," as they were called, would be numbered 294-1, and each subsequent reading would increase the dash number (294-2, 294-3, and so on). Whenever a reading is referenced in this book, it will be followed by the reading number. Since quotes from the readings are usually only a small part of the reading given (some readings can include several pages of material), different quotes can have the same reading number. Some numbers refer to groups of people, such as the first "Study Group," (series 262); and some numbers refer to specific research or guidance readings, such as the 254 series, containing the "Work" readings dealing with the overall work of the nonprofit organization founded by Cayce (the Association for Research and Enlightenment), and the 364 and 996 series containing the readings given on Atlantis. His psychic discourses were termed "readings," because it was believed that he was "reading" sources. Among the sources read were the minds of the questioners, the Akashic Records (also known as "The Book of Life"), the so-called *collective unconsciousness*, and even God's all-knowing mind, which he referred to as the *Universal Consciousness*.

It was August 10, 1923, before anyone thought to ask the "sleeping" Cayce for insights beyond physical health—questions about life, death, and human destiny and origins. In a small hotel room in Dayton, Ohio, Arthur Lammers asked the first set of philosophical questions that were to lead to an entirely new way of using Cayce's strange abilities. It was during this line of questioning that Cayce first began to talk about reincarnation as though it were as real and natural as the functioning of a physical body. This shocked and challenged Cayce and his family. They were deeply religious people, doing this work to help others, because that's what their Christian faith taught. As a child, Cayce began to read the Bible from front to back, and did so every year of his adult life. Reincarnation was not part of the Cayce family's reality. Yet, the healings and help continued to come, so the Cayce family continued with the physical material, but cautiously reflected on the strange philosophical material. Ultimately, the Cayce's began to accept the ideas, though not as "reincarnation" per se. Edgar Cayce preferred to call it, "The Continuity of Life." He felt that the Bible did contain much evidence that life, the true life in the Spirit, is continual. And if there is life after death—the life of the soul—well, then it's just a short step for the soul to also have life before birth. In fact, he found that deep in the lore of Christianity, the "preexistence of the soul" was an accepted truth, one that explained how free-willed souls incarnate into such varying circumstances. If God created all souls equally, then it stands to reason that each soul had previously used their free will, which in turn brought about their present circumstances. He read in the Bible where Jesus' disciples revealed their belief in preexistence when they asked Jesus, "Master, who did sin, this man, or his parents, that he was born blind?" (John 9:2, King James Version [KJV]) The only way the blind man could have sinned and been born blind was if his soul had existed prior to his birth. This helped Cayce and his family tolerate the strange idea of reincarnation and karma.

Eventually, Edgar Cayce, following advice from his own readings, moved to Virginia Beach, Virginia, and set up a hospital where he continued to conduct his "Physical Readings" for the health of others. But he also continued this new line of readings called "Life Readings." From 1925 through 1944, he conducted some 2,500 Life Readings, describing the past lives of individuals as casually as if everyone understood that reincarnation was a fact. Such subjects as deep-seated fears, mental blocks, vocational talents, innate urges and abilities, marriage difficulties, child training, etc., were examined in the light of what the readings called the "karmic patterns" resulting from previous lives experienced by the individual's soul.

When he died on January 3, 1945, in Virginia Beach, he left 14,306 documented stenographic records of the telepathic–clairvoyant readings he had given for more than 6,000 different people over a period of forty–three years, consisting of 49,135 pages, and more than 24 million words. Of the 14,306 readings, 9,603 were health readings.

The readings constitute one of the largest and most impressive records of psychic perception. Together with their relevant records, correspondence, and reports, they have been cross–indexed into thousands of subject headings and placed at the disposal of doctors, psychologists, students, writers, and investigators who still come to examine them. Of course, they are also available to the general public in books or the complete volume of the readings on DVD–Rom, as well as in an online database (see EdgarCayce.org/membership).

The nonprofit known as the Association for Research and Enlightenment (A.R.E.) was founded by Cayce in 1931 to preserve, research, and share these readings. As an open–membership organization, it continues to index and catalog the information, initiate investigation and experiments, and conduct conferences, seminars, and lectures, and operate online courses and study groups. The association also conducts tours each year to various sacred sites around the world. The Virginia Beach headquarters is host to thousands of visitors each year from all around the world who come to tour the campus, attend conferences, visit the bookstore, or explore the library—one of the largest metaphysical libraries in the world with more than 65,000 volumes.

The Cayce work has grown to include the Edgar Cayce Foundation (the readings preservation and archiving arm of the organization), Atlantic University (a graduate–level, online university), and the Cayce/ Reilly® School of Massage. There is also an A.R.E. summer camp in the Blue Ridge Mountains of Virginia. The A.R.E. has a large website with an enormous amount of free information at EdgarCayce.org. The address of the headquarters is Edgar Cayce's A.R.E., 215 67th Street, Virginia Beach, VA 23451 USA, and they can be reached via telephone at 757–428–3588, or 800–333–4499 (toll–free in the U.S. and Canada).

1

❧◉☙

Don't Look Beyond Yourself

We have a natural inclination to look outside of ourselves for the supernatural world. It is not out here. Well it is, but it is not visible. And it's important to recognize that those who "see" the supernatural do not have additional parts to their eyes that you and I lack. Our physical eyes are virtually the same as theirs. We all see by the functioning of two types of photoreceptors in our retinas: rods and cones. We have roughly 120 million supersensitive rods and 6 to 7 million color-sensitive cones. Every healthy human has this arrangement. Normally we only see things that are within a very narrow range of the electromagnetic spectrum (the EM spectrum). This range includes less than five percent of the entire EM spectrum. When energy frequencies within the "visible light" spectrum strike our retina, electrochemical impulses are created that are transmitted to the area of our brain responsible for vision. A pattern in the visual cortex is created by these electrochemical impulses that imitate the visible light pattern striking the retina. Energy outside of this narrow range produces no response

1

from the retina's rods and cones. We normally see wavelengths from red to violet. But some creatures see frequencies on the outer edges of our visible light spectrum, namely *infra*-red and *ultra*-violet. For example, owls, hawks, and eagles perceive *infrared* frequencies—that is, they can perceive the energy waves created by *heat*. Bees, reindeer, sockeye salmon, and many birds perceive *ultraviolet* frequencies. Curiously, butterflies, which are often associated with fairies and the fairy kingdom, are considered by researchers to have the widest visual range of any creature!

Those who see the supernatural or, more likely, saw it when they were very young, were using the same eyes that you and I have; the only difference is—or was—their *consciousness*. A mind that is completely structured around the universe of matter only sees matter. A mind that is open to seeing, or probably more correctly, *perceiving*, the *energy* in all matter and particles will likely perceive these. Without getting too deeply into quantum field theory, it is helpful to understand how "fields" and matter interact and coexist. Every particle exists in a field related to that particle, and particles cannot exist without a field, *but* fields can exist without a particle (such as the Higgs field). And this is where the visible and invisible worlds coexist—and where supernatural entities like angels and fairies live. They only occasionally express themselves in visible form. Perceiving angels, fairies, and the other normally invisible life forms is about *expanded* consciousness.

The paradox in achieving this necessary consciousness is that it is approached from *within* us. It is found through a *shift* in our usual consciousness and our normal perception. Since our physical self considers all life to be out here in physicality, we miss the angels, fairies, and other invisibles—unless they intentionally manifest themselves within our visual range of perception. The way to the supernatural is through perception *beyond* physical matter. Our physical, carnal eyes and ears are not designed to perceive non-physical entities and energies. But we do have *within* us the ability to perceive the supernatural if our mind expands our range.

In Edgar Cayce's volumes, we find some seventy-two discourses on "the unseen forces" and how much more of an influence they are in our lives than the seen. Cayce explained that seeing the unseen requires "a consciousness of that divine force that emanates in Life itself in this material plane." (281-7)

Consider this: All the stars, planets, and galaxies that can be detected throughout the entire, infinite universe make up only *four percent* of the universe! Four percent! The other ninety–six percent is made up of substances that cannot be seen or easily explained. These invisible sub–stances are called "dark energy" and "dark matter" ("dark" here means *unseen* and *undetected*, not evil). Astronomers base the existence of dark matter on the gravitational influence that it exerts on "normal matter" (or the parts of the universe that can be seen). Let's just consider this a bit further; our universe may contain as many as 100 *billion* galaxies, *each* with billions of stars, massive clouds of gas and dust, countless planets and moons, and enormous amounts of cosmic debris—yet everything that we detect is only four percent of the total mass and energy in the universe!

Perceiving the whole requires an *inner* shift in perception, not better eyes and ears. Expanding our consciousness is the key to seeing and hearing the supernatural realms of angels and fairies, and the like. Cayce teaches, " . . . the fairies and those of every form that do not give expression in a material way . . . are only seen by those who are attuned to the infinite." (2547–1) Attuned to the infinite?

From the time he was a very young boy, Edgar Cayce could see fairies, sprites, angels, and invisible friends. He could see discarnate souls among the incarnate. He could hear them and talk to them. He explained that it was like having a switch in his head—a switch that he could flip on in order to see ghosts and communicate with them. He also saw auras around the bodies of incarnate people. These auras emanated colors and patterns that gave him insight into the person's mental, emotion, and spiritual condition, even as it changed during a conversation. Here are a few examples from his readings:

[An] aura is the emanation, or the influence that is ever present with an animate body, that may change or alter as to that which is the impelling influence of or about same—or from within . . . Aura changes, to be sure, [according] to the temperament.   282-4

The aura, then, is the emanation that arises from the very vibratory influences of an individual entity mentally, spiritually—especially of the spiritual forces.   319-2

Hence we find in the aura the physical and the mental and spiritual emanations, that show for developments and retardments as well as abilities for the studying, classifying and applying of same.

1612-1

(Q) Am I beginning to see auras?
(A) Beginning to see auras. As life, light, and love—with understanding—is reflected in self, so may there be seen those of the same reflection from others.
(Q) What is the significance of the flashes and forms which I frequently see?
(A) Those of the higher vibrations of inter-between, as well as spiritual forces taking forms in or before the mental self.   281-4

See how he said "taking forms in or before the mental self"? That's the difference between seeing with carnal eyes and seeing with an expanded consciousness in the mental self. The mind is the true perceiver of angels, fairies, and the invisibles. Actually, in truth, the brain–mind is the perceiver of everything that strikes the retinas, and a more open mind perceives more than physical matter.

Cayce's wife, Gertrude, shared a story about the two of them asleep on the *second* floor of their home when someone tapped on the bedroom window! Edgar immediately knew who this spirit was and went downstairs to let the ghost in. He explained that she needed help finding her way to the next life, because she had died recently and was lost as to what she should do and where she should be. She knew Mr. Cayce would know, but having arrived at his home after he and his wife had retired, she simply tapped on their bedroom window rather than enter into their private space.

From Edgar Cayce's perspective, "For Spirit is the natural, the normal condition of an entity." (816–10) Spirit is our normal, natural condition! Think about this for a moment. Here we are in these physical bodies with our personalities and friends and families, and all our incarnate life history, and from his deep trance state he is telling us that our "natural, normal condition" is as a spirit—a ghost! Our normal condition is as a mind/energy being, and we are temporarily in a physical body. The life essence and deeper consciousness make up our more natural state as an immortal soul. According to Cayce's teachings, we originally were, and remain today, *celestial* beings who are only *temporarily* living a *terrestrial* life in this reality.

> For the soul is eternal and if the entity will analyze its own self, it is body, mind and soul. Soul [is that] which longs for spiritual interpretations, mental understanding and physical harmony and rest. These are parts of the experience of every soul.   5330-1

Despite our more natural, normal condition of being spirit, our soul's incarnation into this life is intentional and with purpose, a purpose that helps our soul grow through living what we believe to be ideal or of the best. We have a tip from Jesus on how to gain awareness of our souls: "In your patience possess ye your souls." (Luke 21:19, KJV) And Cayce agrees: "A patience . . . may be found when the oneness of purpose, oneness of ideal, are correlated in life, light *and* the immortal things of life experiences in the earth." (2938-1) The immortal things of life may be found while incarnate in this world through a oneness of purpose that brings patience, and patience awakens our soul with all its perceptive abilities—such as seeing angels, fairies, and the normally invisible. Our soul and its mind have the extra-sensory perception to see the invisible realms of life and the beings that inhabit them. Cayce taught that the seemingly psychic senses necessary to see and hear angels, fairies, sprites, brownies, gnomes, leprechauns, the "little people," elves, spirits, and for that matter the souls of passed-on loved ones, are the *natural* senses of the soul! (3744-2) The more we become awakened to our soul, our spirit, the more we *naturally* see and hear beyond the rigidly physical world. In this same discourse, Cayce explains that our soul and its mind can and will use the five senses of our body's as well as its psychic-senses.

Almost as important as our having a greater capacity to see the invisible is the comfort felt by the invisibles when we approach them with *an awakened soul and mind*. More on how we may develop greater perception will be covered in Chapter 10.

2

⚜

Angels and the Heavens

hese days, many of us think that there is *one* heaven and *two* types of angelic beings: angels and archangels. But it was not considered so in classical times when it was believed there were seven heavens and nine different "choirs" or "orders" of angels, each composed of distinctly different angelic beings. Let's explore the *classical* view of the heavens and angels.

The Heavens

"In the beginning, God created the heavens and the earth." (Genesis 1:1) (Here "heavens" is the Hewbrew word *shamayim*, which has a dual meaning comparable in English to "the lofts" or "lofty places," likely referring to the dual realms of the visible sky and then the ether of celestial regions beyond the sky. Most every translation of this Bible verse uses the plural "heavens" except for the King James.) In all trans–lations of the Bible, this opening line clearly indicates that there are *heavens*, not simply *a* heaven. We acknowledge this in our language; for example, when a person says, "I was in seventh heaven," he means that he was the happiest he could be, because the seventh heaven is the highest heaven in lore and legend. The mystical Jewish texts that make up the Kabbalah *detail* these seven heavens and give insight into how one may traverse them while incarnate in this world. In other words, one does not have to die to experience the heavens. The disciple Paul revealed this when he wrote, "I know a man in Christ who fourteen years ago . . . was caught up even to the third heaven." (II Corinthians, 12:2) Paul was speaking of himself about an experience he had while incarnate.

In Kabbalah's *Merkabah* mysticism—based on the visions of Ezekiel, Isaiah, and Daniel and found in *Hekhalot* writings—these teachings instruct how one may ascend to and through the heavens by meditative practices, passing from one level of heaven to another, finally entering through the "seven palaces" in the "seventh heaven" to the very "throne of God."

Curiously, Cayce's metaphysical discourses agree with the teachings of Merkabah. This name means "chariots" and is a metaphor for heavenly "vehicles" that enable us to make passage through the heavens. The ancient Egyptians had the same concept but used boats to traverse the heavens. In the following Cayce discourse, the three–dimensional imagery of chariots shifts to fourth–dimensional *states of consciousness*. An angelic being is speaking through Cayce's trance–state body. Notice how the angelic being uses a three–dimensional object, "the Throne," but then gives the fourth–dimensional description: "threshold of Universal Consciousness." Here's the Cayce discourse:

> . . . *no one approaches the Throne—or the threshold of universal consciousness—without that purpose of either lifting self to that consciousness or bringing us [heavenly angels] down to their own ideal . . . Then why, even I [a heavenly angel], should I make thee falter, or why should one seek less than the Gods of Glory?*
> 311-5

There are two comments in this reading that need elaboration: 1) From the perspective of the angel speaking through or being channeled by Cayce, we are to *lift ourselves up* through the heavens to the "Throne" of God or Universal Consciousness, for the other way—bringing heaven down to us—does not help awaken us to grow toward our destiny with our infinite Creator. 2) This guidance from the angel also touches on the often-ignored teaching that *we are gods*—sons and daughters of the Most High—as written in Psalm 82:6 (KJV): "I have said, Ye are gods, all of you are children of the most High." And even Jesus referred us to this passage by an answer he gave to the Pharisees in the gospel of John 10:33-34 (KJV): "'For a good work we stone thee not; but for blasphemy; and because that thou, being a man, makest thyself God.'" "Jesus answered them, 'Is it not written in your law, I said, Ye are gods?'" Jesus is referring to the line in Psalm 82.

Given our present condition and circumstances, I realize how difficult it is for us to think we could possibly be gods. It may help us if we use the ancient Egyptian term: *godlings*. We are godlings of the great God; the one supreme God conceived us in His/Her *image* as recorded in chapter one of Genesis: "And God said, 'Let us make man in our image, after our likeness . . . ' And so God created man in his own image, in the image of God created he him; male and female created he them." (Genesis 1:26-27, KJV) Of course this was *not* the physical creation of our bodily existence that came later in chapter 2: "And the Lord God formed man of the dust of the ground, and breathed into his nostrils the breath of life; and man became a living soul." (Genesis 2:7, KJV)

Cayce addresses the challenges we face in making passage from this world or level of consciousness to the higher dimensions of awareness, the *heavenly* realms:

> Passing from the material consciousness to a spiritual or cosmic . . . oft does an entity or being not become conscious of that about it; much in the same manner as an entity born into the material plane only becomes conscious gradually of that designated as time and space for the material or third dimensional plane. In the passage the entity becomes conscious . . . of being in a fourth or higher dimensional plane takes place, much in the same way as the consciousness is gained in the material. For, as we have given, that we see manifested in the material plane is but a shadow of that in the spiritual plane.   5749-3

It was teachings like this one from Edgar Cayce that encouraged me to budget time in my incarnate life to practice and experience the higher dimensions, and from my early twenties I have used Cayce, ancient Eastern, and Kabbalistic methods and concepts to become conscious of making passage through the heavens without losing touch with my life and relationships in this world. And just as Cayce said, we awaken to the higher, heavenly dimensions in the same way that we awaken to a more expanded consciousness of this world. As to the *nature* of perception in the higher dimensions, Cayce explains that this plane of existence is like a "shadow" of the invisible realms: "There is no difference in the unseen world to that that is visible, save in the unseen so much greater expanse or space may be covered!" (5754-3) My experiences with the higher dimensions is just as Cayce indicated; they feel more *expansive* than the physical world, more open, and my spirit/mind seems to move through them easily and quickly. Many others have had the same experiences with the nonphysical dimensions. It's a shift in consciousness, in perception, from finite to infinite, from an individual to a universal. This is one reason why so many meditators describe feeling a profound *oneness* with *all* life when in deep meditation. Aloneness or individualness dissolves into collectiveness and universalness.

When Cayce talked about *soul* travel—not bodily travel—he described the three-dimensional objects—planets, stars, and the like—as "shadows" of their higher-dimensional condition. In Cayce's trance-state perception, our solar system is a physical expression of *mental* and *spiritual* realities. Here's an example:

> As an entity passes on . . . from this present [time] or this solar system, this sun, these forces, it passes through the various spheres— leading first into that central force . . . known as Arcturus [this star is Cayce's "star gate" in and out of our solar system]—nearer the Pleiades—on and on—through the eons of time, as called—or space . . . [Eventually, an entity passes] into the inner forces, inner sense, then may they again—after a period of nearly ten thousand years . . . enter into the earth to make manifest those forces gained in its passage. In entering, [the entity] takes on those forms that may be known in the dimensions of that plane which it occupies, there being not only three dimensions—as of the Earth—but there

may be seven, in Mercury—or four, in Venus—or five, as in Jupiter. There may be only one as in Mars. There may be many more as in those of Neptune, or they may become even as nil—until purified in Saturn's fires.   311-2

Keep in mind that he is not talking about landing on the *physical* surface of these planets but rather entering their higher dimensional realms of consciousness, vibration, and non-physical existence. Think of our world and our condition here as H_2O in solid form or ice, and then the next highest realms or heavens are like H_2O in a more fluid, liquid form, and the even higher realms are as H_2O in vaporous or cloud-like forms. This may help us get some sense of how a being can exist in *different* conditions—solid, liquid, and vapor—and yet retain its fundamental essence, H_2O in this example. These conditions of H_2O are comparable to physical, mental, and spiritual conditions: solid, liquid, and vapor.

Let's continue. Cayce identifies our soul's *motivation* as follows:

"As [the entity] moves from sphere to sphere, [it] seeks its way to the home, to the face of the Creator, the Father, the first cause." (136–83) Cayce identifies the first cause as: ". . . that the created would be the companion for the Creator." This is the reason we were created, and as a result, the created (our soul) is given opportunities to "show itself to be not only worthy of, but companionable to, the Creator." (5753–1) Now we should realize that we are talking about being companionable to the Creator of the entire universe, so we do not want to be boring companions! For this reason, our souls are well motivated to explore, learn, and grow!

As I mentioned earlier and wrote about in my book *Edgar Cayce and the Kabbalah*, there are Kabbalah texts teaching one how to ascend through the "heavenly palaces" (*Hekhalot* means "palaces of heaven") and what the experience will be in these various non-physical palaces or realms of the seven heavens. There are also Kabbalah texts teaching how one may draw down angelic spirits to interact with us. Cayce's readings are not against this, but they encourage us to let God send the guides and angels, for God knows best, and we have a tendency to attract the wrong energies, or at least the lesser ones. Cayce's instruction would be to ask God to send angelic help rather than attempt to evoke such with our own will and desire. And whenever possible, Cayce encourages us

to *lift* our minds and hearts up into the heavens rather than draw entities down from heaven—just as the channeled angel instructed earlier.

There are several larger documents of the Hekhalot texts, such as
Hekhalot Rabbati (in which six of the seven palaces of God are described),
Hekhalot Zutarti, Shiur Komah, and *3 Khanokh* (which is also known as
3 Enoch, and contains "The Book of the Palaces," "The Book of Rabbi
Ishmael the High Priest," and "The Revelation of Metatron"). There are
also hundreds of small documents, many little more than fragments,
which address the concept of heavenly realms (palaces, firmaments, and
planes) and describe methods for traversing them (though this is very
dangerous and requires much practice and skill—as well as a pure heart
and a focused and shielded mind). I'll describe these in a moment.

The meditative journey through the seven heavens was also known
and practiced among various Gnostic groups and some early Chris-
tians—often in secret. As I wrote earlier and bears repeating, it would
appear that the disciple Paul had made this passage: "I know a man in
Christ, fourteen years ago (whether in the body, I don't know, or whether out of the body, I don't know; God knows), such a one caught up
into the third heaven." (II Corinthians, 12:2) Paul appears to have used
a method in which the Spirit draws us up into a level of Its presence.
In this case, Paul was "caught up" to the third heaven. Notice also that
Paul could not determine if he was in his body or out of it. Out-of-body
experiences are so much a part of our modern culture that we now have
an acronym for them: OBE. But this is not just a modern phenomenon,
it was known back in Paul's time as well, coming from the Greek term
for "self watcher," meaning viewing the surrounding environment from
a position *outside* of one's body. The English word for the original Greek
word is "autoscopy." Also associated with OBE are astral projection
(meaning the separation of the astral body from its connection to the
physical body), soul travel, and spirit walking, even the most modern of
experiences—"near-death experiences" (NDEs)—are among out-of-body
experiences—they are a result of modern medicine's abilities to revive
a dead body under certain circumstances, and the revived person then
describing how they saw their dead body and what the doctors and
nurses did to revive it. Paul experienced one of these transcending
events, and it allowed him to visit, or at least perceive, the third level
of the heavens.

In the Koran, dictated to Mohammed by the archangel Gabriel, it is written, "See you not how Allah [literally in Arabic, "the God"] has created the seven heavens one above another, and made the moon a light in their midst and made the sun a lamp?" (Sura 71)

In most teachings of the Kabbalah, the seven heavens are listed from lowest to highest as follows:

1. Veil (Hebrew, *Vilon*—the curtain, the veil of heaven (*Vilon Shemaim*); taken from Isaiah 40:22, "It is he who sits above the circle of the earth, and earth's inhabitants are like grasshoppers; who stretches out the heavens like a curtain [or veil], and spreads them like a tent to dwell in."

2. Firmament (*Raki'a*—the firmament, the canopy, the expanse of heaven, which are the stars, moon, and sun; mentioned in Gen 1:14–18, "'Let there be lights in the firmament of the heavens to separate the day from the night; and let them be for signs and for seasons and for days and years, and let them be lights in the firmament of the heavens to give light upon the earth.' And it was so. And God made the two great lights, the greater light to rule the day, and the lesser light to rule the night; he made the stars also. And God set them in the firmament of the heavens to give light upon the earth, to rule over the day and over the night, and to separate the light from the darkness. And God saw that it was good."

3. Cloud/Sky (*Shehakim*—the clouds from which the manna from heaven fell to nourish the seekers. Here is where the well of the "water of life" is and the fountain of gardens. These associations are taken from Psalm 78:24–26, "And He commanded the skies above, and opened the doors of heaven; and He caused manna to rain upon them for food," and the "cloud" in 1 Kings 8:10–13, "And when the priests came out of the holy place, a cloud filled the house of the Lord, so that the priests could not stand to minister because of the cloud; for the glory of the Lord filled the house of the Lord. Then Solomon said, 'The Lord has set the sun in the heavens, but has said that he would dwell in thick darkness. I have built thee an exalted house, a place for thee to dwell in forever.'"

4. Mansion (*Zebul*—the lofty dwelling, "mansion of holiness" (*zevul kodshekha*) taken from Psalm 93:5, considered the temple-mansion

in the Golden City. As found in I Kings 8:13, "I have surely built Thee a house of habitation, a place for Thee to dwell in forever. And whence do we derive that it is called heaven?" and in Isaiah 63:15, "Look down from heaven, and see, even from Thy holy and glorious habitation." And Jesus refers to mansions in John 14:1–4, "In my Father's house are many mansions: if it were not so, I would have told you. I go to prepare a place for you. And if I go and prepare a place for you, I will come again, and receive you unto myself; that where I am, there ye may be also. And whither I go ye know, and the way ye know." Now Thomas challenges this, telling Jesus that they do not know where he is going or the way. But we do; and we have to go back to an answer Jesus gave Nicodemus to understand how this could be: "No one has ascended into heaven but he/she who descended from heaven, even the Son of man." (John 3:13) We are the children of God, and as such we originated in the heavens, thus our souls descended from the heavens in order to incarnate in this world, and we'll ascend back into heavens after our physical body dies. This is how Jesus can say, you know where I'm going and you know the way.

5. Dwelling (*Ma'on*—the refuge, a place of peace from the struggles. Home of the ministering angels mentioned in Deuteronomy 26:15, "Thy holy habitation."

6. "City of God" (*Makon*—the changeless, perfect residence, containing the template or prototype for all life forms. This is the storehouse of good, eternal treasures. The name is taken from Psalm 46:5–6, "There is a river whose streams make glad the city of God, the holy habitation of the Most High. God is in the midst of her, she shall not be moved; God will help her right early."

7. "Vast Plains of God" (*Aravot*—the highest heaven, the vast expansive plains of Infinity. This is the Divine Womb from which all life originally came into being and to which it returns, as taken from Psalm 68:4–5, "Lift up a song to him who rides upon the infinite plains; his name is the Lord, exult before him! Father of the fatherless and protector of widows is God in his holy habitation."

Notice that the first three heavens are associated with physical life, the second three with mental dimensions of consciousness, and the last with Infinity—a quality that human beings would have difficulty knowing directly because of their finite focus. Yet, through careful passage during deep meditation and transcendent ecstasy, we can rise to levels of consciousness in the Infinite Mind of God.

The most important heaven for us is the lowest one, the Veil or Curtain, because if we can perceive it and develop a conscious awareness of it, then we have made the first big step toward total spiritual awakening. Despite what you may think, we know this veil well and are familiar with the qualities of our mind on both sides of this veil. To use a familiar example, how many times have we had a dream that impressed us (either scared us or inspired us or simply caught our attention), and as we came closer to waking, we noticed that our bladder was full, so we decided to go empty the bladder and then come back to the bed and reflect on the dream? Yet, when we returned to our bed, the dream was completely gone! We had no recollection of it. How is this possible? It is because we just experienced the veil, a most subtle yet opaque veil! When in the dream, we were in our soul mind and were quite comfortable there. We knew it as a part of ourselves. Then, as we engaged our body to walk to the bathroom, we passed through this veil into our outer mind, which is awakened to move the body. However, our *outer* mind did not have the dream! It has no content of the dream, only a sense that the inner mind has content that is going to be reviewed. But it does not contain that content. Now we see just how subtle and yet opaque this veil is. We do not even notice when we pass through it, and yet, once on the other side, we cannot see back through it.

Fortunately, that's only partially true, because if we practice becoming more aware of the subtle aspects of our consciousness, we will come to perceive the movement through the veil and know which side of the veil we are on at any given time.

Now that we have some knowledge of the heavens, let's look into the classical understanding of angels.

The Angels

As crowded and busy as earth is, the heavens are many times more crowded and busy. How many angels are there? Well the apostle John wrote: "I looked and heard the voice of many angels, numbering thousands upon thousands, and ten thousand times ten thousand." (Revelation 5:11, NIV) The study of angels and the doctrine on angels are called Angelology, and were once widely accepted as a serious part of Theology. The term *angel* appears in the Bible 194 to 196 times, depending on which version you're searching. And in some cases, angels are implied and understood by the scholars to be angels even though the term is not used. For example, in Genesis 18:1–2, the Lord appears to Abraham in the form of three "men," which Abraham immediately knew were physical expressions of angels from heaven, and he treated them as such. But for all outward appearances, they looked like men. This is when Abraham debates with the three angels over how many righteous people need to be among the citizens of Sodom and Gomorrah to keep the angels from destroying the cities, finally getting them to agree to ten righteous people.

As to the appearance of angels, even the Scriptures warn us that sometimes we "entertained angels unawares." (Hebrews 13:2, KJV)

Let's begin our study with Edgar Cayce's comments on angels.

(Q) Is the guardian angel a healing force for physical betterment? (A) The guardian angel—that is the companion of each soul as it enters into a material experience—is ever an influence for the keeping of that attunement between the creative energies or forces of the soul-entity *and* health, life, light and immortality. Thus, to be sure, it is a portion of that influence for *healing* forces.

And as may be experienced in the activities of individuals, it may become so accentuated as to be the greater influence in their experience. Thus it is as has been given of old; that to some there is the gift of healing, to some the gift of speech, interpreting of tongues, to ministering. Yet all are of the same Spirit. For these are ever that which is the assurance, in that as has been given—God hath not willed that any soul should perish but hath with every temptation, with every condition prepared an association, an activity, a manner, a way for the regeneration of those influences or forces that may cause the overcoming of fear or any of those things that would separate a soul from the Creative Forces.

Hence, as has been indicated for this body here, the making of the physical adjustments is necessary; but it is just as necessary for the activities of the associations through which the energies of the bodily forces may be attuned to the spiritual and mental self—through the closer association and walk with creative energies within self.

For all must coordinate. Just as in the Godhead—Father, Son, Holy Spirit—so within self: Body, Mind, Soul. Mind is the Builder; Mind is the Way—as the Christ-Consciousness. As it is directed then through the influences of the bodily functions it becomes aware of its oneness, and thus is the guardian force made to be at-one with the whole of the purposes and desires, and the will of the individual.

Do these things then, as we find, as indicated, and we will bring to the physical forces a better cooperation and coordination; and thus through the mental application of the at-onement with the Creative Forces, better reactions in every manner.

(Q) Is it through the guardian angel that God speaks to the individual?
(A) Ever through that influence or force as He has given, "Ye abide in me and I in thee, as the Father abides in me, so may we make our abode with thee."

Then as the guardian influence or angel is ever before the face of the Father, through same may that influence ever speak—but only by the command of or attunement to that which is thy ideal.

What then is thy ideal? In *whom* have ye believed, as well as in what have ye believed? Is that in which thou hast believed able to keep ever before thee that thou committest unto Him?

Yes—through thy angel, through thy self that is the angel—does the self speak with thy Ideal! 1646-1

Notice this last line, because it reinforces the teaching that we are of Divine origin and, despite our present physical condition, we remain connected to our Creator through an unseen portion of our being that is angelic: "through thy self that is the angel."

Notice also that Cayce ties the angelic portion of our being to our ideal. Again and again Cayce's readings ask us, "What is your ideal?" and "In what and in whom do you believe?" Is it our ideal to be among the children of God or simply the children of men? Do we have room in our hearts and minds for heavenly things? Or is it earthly things that matter most to us? You would not be reading this book if earthly things were all that interested you, so let's assume that you are interested in heavenly things and that these have a place in your ideal life and consciousness.

Cayce reveals that our angel is always in communion with God: "The face of self's *own* angel is ever before the Throne. Commune oft with Him." (1917-1) Jesus affirms this in Matthew's gospel: "Take heed that ye despise not one of these little ones [the children gathered around him]; for I say unto you, that in heaven their angels do always behold the face of my Father which is in heaven." (Matthew 18:10, KJV)

When Edgar Cayce was in the deep trance state through which he obtained readings, his subconscious, or soul mind, could attune to the very highest sources in the spiritual dimensions. In the well-known *A Search for God* study group readings, the 262 series of reading numbers, there were occasions when the archangel Michael would actually speak *through* Cayce and give powerful messages. Cayce's discourses called Michael the archangel of change:

> Michael is the lord of the way—and in the *ways* of understanding, of conception, of bringing about those things that make for the changes in the attitudes in physical, mental, or material relationships . . . [Michael] is the *guide* through such spiritual relations . . .
>
> 585-1

When studied as a whole, the Cayce readings indicate that each of us is a soul that is learning to become companionable to God and to the other created beings (the two great commandments: love God; love others). On the earthly side of the soul is a temporary outer persona we call the personality, often referred to by Cayce as "the body–mind." This is what you and I consider to be our real self. On the other side of our soul self is a divine portion of our being that is an angel. It is heavenly, has never left its original place with God, and was made in the image of God. This is the "holy immortal" portion of us, as described in Zoroastrian lore. We have a bodily self, a soul self, and an angelic self. These three have three levels of consciousness: conscious mind, subconscious mind (which Cayce describes to be much larger than we currently understand), and superconscious mind.

For an example of how these three portions of our being interface, let's consider the biblical story of the patriarch Jacob, his twin brother, Esau, and the angel as a metaphor for these three parts of ourselves. In personality, Esau was a hunter and warrior, hairy and strong, wild and free, who loved the fields and woods. Jacob, on the other hand, was more internal and reflective in nature. He was gentle, enjoyed learning and good conversation, liked the company of women and the surroundings of the tribal camp, and had developed a skill with domesticated animals, particularly husbandry of breeding healthy goats and sheep. Esau symbolizes our outer self as he sought to experience physical life with as much gusto as possible, whereas Jacob symbolizes our soul self, as he sought to experience the inner, ethereal things, more of the mind and heart than of the body. One night, in a profound experience, Jacob met an angel. He caught firm hold of the angel and would not let the angel go until the angel blessed him. After the blessing, Jacob asked the angel's name, but the angel was surprised by such a question and gave no answer. Could it be that the angel was none other than Jacob's divine self, his angelic self, and that's why he was surprised that Jacob did not already know his name? After this experience, Jacob said that he had seen God "face to face." How could he make such a statement unless the angel was also before the throne of God? We may consider this story to be an example of how our personality, soul, and angel self interact with one another.

The early Christian theologian and philosopher Augustine wrote, "Every visible thing in this world is put under the charge of an angel." The *Genesis Rabba* (a Jewish commentary on the biblical Genesis) states, "There's not a stalk on earth that has not its angel in heaven." According to Psalm 91:9–12 (Revised Standard Version [RSV]): "Because you have made the Lord your refuge, the Most High your habitation, no evil shall befall you, no scourge come near your tent; for he will give his angels charge of you to guard you in all your ways. On their hands they will bear you up, lest you dash your foot against a stone." And as Jesus experienced in Matthew 4:11 (RSV) when he had completed the three challenges by Satan, and was weary, thirsty, and hungry: "Then the devil left him, and behold, angels came and ministered to him." And in Matthew 26:53 (RSV), when he ordered Peter to put his sword away: "Do you think that I cannot appeal to my Father, and he will at once send me more than twelve legions of angels?" God has charged his angels to watch over us, and we can call on this help.

There was a time when only our angelic selves existed. The angelic part of our being was alive and active long before Earth, long before physical bodies. Life existed in the spirit, or we might say, in pure energy without matter. Perhaps, if we think of ourselves as minds without form, this may help awaken us to our angelic portion. The One Mind created within itself many individual minds and gave them free will. Life went along in this manner for many, many eons before some of these angelic beings took form in bodies. What was it like back then? What were the angels doing? Cayce and Kabbalah, along with many earth legends and fables, give us some of the amazing pre–Earth history. Let's explore some of the chronicles of the angels.

In the Old Testament, Yahweh is called "the Lord of hosts;" *hosts* being the legions of angels. Psalm 82:1 (American KJV) states that "God stands in the congregation of the mighty; He judges among the gods." Here the angels compose the congregation and are gods within the one God. Notice that the term *Congregation of God* implies that all in the congregation are godlike, made in the image of God.

When speaking of angelic beings, the Bible uses the terms "messenger of God" (*melakh Elohim*), "messenger of the Lord" (*melakh Adonai*), "Sons of God" (*b'nai Elohim*), and the "Holy Ones" (*ha-qodeshim*). Other terms are used in later texts, such as "the upper ones" (*ha'oleevoneem*).

Metatron is considered the highest of the angels in Kabbalistic mysticism. Metatron is briefly mentioned in the Talmud and figures prominently in Merkabah mystical texts. In 3 Enoch, or the Book of Heavenly Palaces (*Sefer Hekhalot*), there is a link between Enoch (son of Jared who was great–grandfather of Noah) and his *transformation into* the angel Metatron. Surprisingly, there is the same connection in the Edgar Cayce readings! As strange as the name is, this is the highest angel in almost all listings of angels.

Michael, who serves as a warrior and an advocate for Israel (Daniel 10:13), is considered to be the guardian angel of the Israelites; and Gabriel is the guardian angel of the Ishmaelites (modern–day Arabs). This began with the two sons of Abraham: Isaac and Ishmael. Gabriel is mentioned in the book of Daniel (8:15–17) and briefly in the Talmud, as well as in many Merkabah mystical texts. And Daniel's visions name the archangel Michael—which is the first time in the Bible that an angel's name is spoken.

Seraphim and Cherubim

In Jewish and Dionysian lore, the Congregation of Angels is arranged into two main choirs: Seraphim and Cherubim.

Seraphim are the highest order of angels and attend to the throne and altar of God. They are variously referred to as the "burning ones," the "red ones," and "beings of fire," because of their association with the fire on the altar of God and the fire of truth, particularly the "test as by fire" that the archangel Michael requires of every soul who attempts to pass to higher levels of heaven. In the Bible, seraphs (mentioned only in Isaiah 6:2 and 6:6) surround the throne of God and bring Isaiah a coal from the fire on the altar of God with which to cleanse his lips and speech.

Seraphs are often depicted with six wings. The colors red and white are associated with them, as well as the element of fire. Cayce's reading 275–35 actually refers to the "Seraphim choir" when instructing a young man about his music training, noting that the "Prince of Peace was a harpist" in the Seraphim choir.

Cherubim, on the other hand, are mentioned throughout the Bible. Their name is derived from the Assyrian (or Akkadian) word *kirubu*, which means "one who prays, blesses, or intercedes," and are often seen as those who intercede between God and humans. As the second order of angels, they are often depicted as winged children, but this originated during the Middle Ages and is not an original image for them. Cherubs are depicted as having four wings, and blue is the color associated with them, because of their connection with the sky and, in some cases, with the wind and the element of air.

Cayce's readings portray the angels as *active* beings, much involved with the lives of humans. They were and are co-creators with the Creator, and as such, created much of the universe that we see. How many angels were created? According to the Egyptians, each star in heaven is the light of one angel, and there are more stars in the portion of the universe that is visible from earth than there are grains of sand on all the beaches and deserts of earth!

The Nine Choirs or Orders of Angelic Beings

The traditional order of the angelic hierarchy fits with the three Triads of the Tree of Life in Kabbalah (Celestial, Moral, and Mundane), and in each of the three Triads are three choirs of angels. Here is the order:

First Choirs
Seraphim
Cherubim
Thrones

Second Choirs
Dominations (Dominions)
Virtues
Powers

Third Choirs
Principalities
Archangels
Angels

• The Seraphim are the highest order of the nine orders of angels. They surround the throne of God continually singing, "Holy, Holy, Holy is the God of Hosts!" They are said to be so bright that humans cannot look at them. Lucifer was among the Seraphim before the rebellion in heaven that led to his fall and that of many angels. The Prince of this choir is Michael.

• The Cherubim were God's choice for the Ark of the Covenant. Dionysius the Areopagite (judge of the Areopagus, in the biblical book of Acts 17:34) wrote much about the lore of angels, and he taught that these were the angels of knowing or knowledge. They were assigned to guard the Tree of Life from humanity, less we eat from it and become physically immortal rather than spiritually so. (Genesis 3:24, in the Revelation 22:14 this restriction is rescinded, allowing spiritualized humans to eat the fruit of the Tree of Life.) Cherubim are humanlike in appearance and are guardians of God's glory. In Muslim lore, the

Cherubim were formed from Michael's tears over the sins of the Faithful. They are alluded to as celestial attendants in the Revelation (chapters 4–6). The Prince of the Cherub Choir is Gabriel.

• The Thrones represent God's divine justice. Dionysius wrote, "It is through the Thrones that God brings His justice upon us." This third choir is known as the "many–eyed ones" because, when viewed by humans, they are covered with eyes. They are known for their humility and submission to God's will. They reside in the area of the cosmos where material form begins to take shape. The lower choirs of angels need the Thrones in order to access God. The Prince of the Thrones is Orifiel, the angel of Saturday and the planet Saturn. He is also Chief of Talismans.

• The Dominions are considered the "Angels of Leadership." Dionysius wrote that theirs is the position of authority, regulating the duties of the angels and making known the commands of God. "Through them the majesty of God is manifested." The Prince of the Dominions is Zadkiel, angel of the fourth emanation of Mercy and Lovingkindness on the Kabbalah Tree of Life.

• The Virtues are known as the "Spirits of Motion" and control the elements (more on this in the chapter on the Elementals). Some refer to them as "the shining ones." They govern Nature. They have control over the seasons, stars, moon, and sun. They are also in charge of and perform miracles, and provide courage, grace, and valor. The fifth choir of angels acts on the orders of the Dominions and represents the power of God. The Prince of the Choir of Virtues is Uzziel, one of the principal angels in rabbinic angelology. According to the *Sepher Rezial Hemelack: The Book of the Angel Rezial*, Uzziel is among the seven angels who stand before the throne of Glory.

• The Powers are warrior angels who fight against evil and defend the heavens and earth. They fight against evil spirits who attempt to bring chaos into the harmony of life. The Prince of this choir is Kamael (also, Camael). In Druid mythology, Kamael is the Angel of War.

• The Principalities is the seventh choir in the hierarchy of angels. Surprisingly, they have hostility toward God and, not so surprisingly, toward humans owing to sin, which is disharmony and imbalance in the Cosmos. The chaos that has come from sin or disharmony has made them upset and harsh in their judgment. The disciple Paul writes that

Christ has gained ultimate rule over them by virtue of his sacrifice in conquering sin and death. (Romans 8:38; 1 Corinthians 15:24; Ephesians 1:21, 3:10, 6:12; Colossians 1:16, 2:10, 15) According to Milton in *Paradise Lost* (VI, p. 447), the Prince of the Choir of Principalities is Nisroch ("the great eagle"), considered by some to be a demon, continuing the idea that the Principalities are hostile. Of course, some of these descriptions reflect a fear of the angels in both humans and fallen angels.

• Archangels are the predominant type of angels mentioned in the Bible (some examples include Jude 1:9 and 1 Thessalonians 4:16). In Greek, "archangel" literally means "chief angel." The archangels are God's messengers to the people at critical times. (Tobit 12:6, 15; John 5:4; Revelation 12:7) The Prince of the archangels is none other than Metatron.

• The ninth choir is the Choir of Angels, which includes our personal guardian angels, who stand before the throne of God and present our petitions while also watching over us, less we stumble on our way to reunion with our Creator. The Prince of this choir is Phaleg, or Phalec, the governing spirit of Mars, often referred to as the "War Lord." Phaleg's signet is among the amulets and talismans worn for protection.

No biblical writer wrote as much about angels and their choirs as Paul. In fact, most of the Bible does not mention much about angels until Paul's letters in the New Testament. In these we learn of the Principalities and Archangels and the names of several angels. Fortunately, there is so much literature beyond the Bible on angels that volumes could be written about the angels and their choirs. As I quoted earlier, Paul himself writes that before his ministry, he ascended (in his body or out of it, he was not sure) to the third heaven, into Paradise, and learned much of what he would subsequently write about.

A significant angel in Edgar Cayce's volumes is Halaliel. In my search of angelic texts, I could not find any angel named Halaliel. However, it is common for angels to have many names. For example, Metatron has more than 100 other names! In one very strange Cayce reading (quoted below), I found that some in attendance believed that Cayce was correlating Halaliel with a most famous angel, Haniel, also known as Anael, Hanael, or Aniel. Haniel is an angel in Jewish angelology and is often included in lists as being one of the seven archangels. In this life reading given to an eight-year-old girl, Cayce was attempting to give this soul's planetary sojourns when, according to Gladys Davis (Cayce's stenographer), he paused for a long time. Here is her record of this reading:

> As to the astrological sojourns, we find Venus with [long pause...] Haniel is rather the guide for the entity, for he is the overlord lord—making for experiences in the entity as of one delicate in its choices, making for a disposition tending towards that of finesse, making the most of all the associations; making friendships easily and drawing upon the force and power from those associations in a manner and way that even the entity itself will not—until it has passed through the experiences of making itself at-one with the greater developing force—understand as to how this is done.
>
> 665-1

Haniel (meaning "grace of God") is the angel of the month of December and is, according to *A Theological Discourse of Angels*, the "governor of Capricorn and Venus." Haniel is the angel who carried Enoch from Earth to Heaven (Enoch did not die, but was "taken by God," Genesis 5:24 and Hebrews 11:5). Haniel is compared with Ishtar, the Chaldean angel who rules Venus. He is an archangel and is listed among the ten holy *sefirot*.

Archangels of the Emanations (the Holy sefirot)

A *sefira* (plural, *sefirot*) is an original *emanation* of God's *holy being* during the creation of the universe. In Kabbalah, there are ten holy and ten unholy sefiroth. The holy ones emanated from God's right side, and the unholy from His left. Some writers compare the ten holy sefiroth to Plato's powers or intelligences, and with the Gnostic's *aeons* or light emanations.

As angels, the holy sefiroth are arranged in this order: Metatron (crown), Raziel (wisdom), Zaphkiel (understanding), Zadkiel (mercy), Kamael (might), Michael (beauty), Haniel (victory), Raphael (splendor), Gabriel (foundation), and Metatron (kingdom). Notice that Metatron is both the first and the last in this listing, which echoes Paul's writing of the first Adam and the last Adam: "The first man Adam became a living soul. The last Adam became a life–giving spirit." (1 Corinthians 15:45) [Note: In some schools, Michael is Splendor and Raphael is Beauty, which does seem to fit better with the meaning of their respective names and roles.]

• Metatron (crown and kingdom) is called King of the Angels, Angel of the Covenant, Prince of the Presence, and the Lesser Yahweh (the *Tetragrammaton*, which is YHWH, the name of the Almighty Father in Heaven). Many believe this name reveals his role as the Logos, God's primary expression into the creation. As the Logos, or "the Word" in the opening lines of John's gospel, Metatron is the bridge between humanity and divinity. He is identified with Mercury, Hermes (Egyptian Thoth), Enoch, and several other key figures, all of which Cayce's readings identify as incarnations of the Logos, the Messiah. There is even a Kabbalistic connection between Adam (before he sinned) and Metatron, a connection that Cayce's readings also make. Kabbalah holds that Metatron was the guiding angel of Israel during the forty–year exodus in the wilderness searching for the Promised Land.

The origin of his strange name is unknown, and it is unusual among Hebrew names. Though difficult to give meaning to, some believe the name comes from the Latin *metator*, meaning "a measurer," which would certainly fit with Hermes/Thoth, who measured the weight of every soul's heart to see if it was light enough to enter the heavens, and then recorded the finding in the Scroll, or Book of Life. Metatron maintains "the Archives of Metatron." In Jewish angelology, it was Metatron who stayed the hand of Abraham, keeping him from killing his son Isaac as a sacrificial offering to God. Metatron resides in the Seventh Heaven, the dwelling place of God. When evoked, he appears as a column of fire, his face as bright as the Sun. In the *Zohar*, he is "the rod of Moses," from which comes life from one side and death from the other. Amazingly, Metatron is the Angel of Death while, at the same time, the Angel of Resurrection! The *Zohar* equates him with Adam before he sinned: pure, powerful, and always in the company of God. Curiously, Metatron is also considered to be the teacher of children who died prematurely.

• Raziel (wisdom) is the legendary author of Kabbalah's *The Book of the Angel (Sefer Raziel)*. His name means "Secret of God." It is said that Noah learned how to build the ark by reading Raziel's tome. Raziel is the Herald of Deity and Preceptor Angel of Adam. According to legend,

Raziel's great power is magic. In *Targum Ecclesiastes* (10, 20), the earliest commentary on the biblical Ecclesiastes, Raziel is the angel that was standing on Mount Horeb proclaiming the secrets to all humanity. In Kabbalah, he is the Chief of the Erelim. The Erelim are the Angels of Peace and are known to weep over destruction and death.

•   Zaphkiel (understanding) is the governor of the planetary realm of Saturn. His name means "Knowledge of God." He is Chief of the Order of Thrones and Ruler of the Order of Cherubim—the angels sent to guard the gates of Eden. Originally they were depicted as the bearers of God's Throne, as the charioteers, and as powerful beings with four wings and four faces. Zaphkiel is also the Herald of Hell, bringing messages to those that have become lost and suffer in their sins.

•   Zadkiel (mercy) is the Angel of Benevolence, Mercy, and Memory, and the Chief of the Order of Dominations. His name means "Righteousness of God." He is ruler of the planetary realm of Jupiter. In the *Zohar*, Zadkiel joins with Zophiel (another name for Zaphkiel) when the archangel Michael goes to battle against the Angels of Darkness. In some lore and magical books, Zadkiel is the Regent of Hell, ruling over lost souls and sinners—as such, it is comforting to know that he is also the angel of mercy.

•   Kamael, often Camael, (strength), meaning "He Who Sees God," is the Chief of the Order of Powers. The Druids considered him the god of war. Naturally, he is the angelic guardian of the planetary realm of Mars (the Roman god of war). He is referred to as "the talisman of the angels"; thus the word *cameo* comes from this angel's name, Camael.

•   Michael (beauty, or some say splendor) is the Chief of Archangels, Protector of the Presence (of God), and Chief of the Order of Virtues. He is the Angel of Repentance, Righteousness, Mercy, and Sanctification. His name means, "Who is as God." He rules the 4th Heaven and is the guardian angel of Israel (but Israel in the sense of all who seek God). He is conqueror of Satan (see 12th chapter of the Revelation). His secret name is Sabbathiel (Lord of the Sabbath, "the intermission"), indicating that when humans rest from their willful doing and when they seek God as opposed to selfish interests, he protects them. His mission, according to Cayce's readings, is as "the lord [or guard] of the Way, *not* the Way but the lord of the Way, hence disputed with the influence of evil. . ." (5749-3)

• Haniel (victory) means Grace of God, Glory of God, or "He Who Sees God." He is Chief of the Order of Principalities and governor of Venus, as was the Chaldean angel Ishtar. His powers were often evoked by the use of an amulet. His name has been found on many ancient amulets.

• Raphael (splendor, or some say beauty) means "God has Healed." He is one of the presences with powers over diseases and wounds that afflict the children of men. He is one of the three angels that Abraham questioned about saving Sodom and Gomorrah (Genesis 18; the other two were believed to be Michael and Gabriel). Legend holds that Raphael handed Noah a book of healing after he landed and was to begin repopulating the world. He is the Angel of the Sun, Prince of the Second Heaven, Chief of the Virtues, Guardian of the Tree of Life, and the Angel of Healing. He is credited as the angel who troubled the healing waters at Bethesda (John 5). This water healed the first to step in it. In The Book of Tobit (a book of the Old Testament Apocrypha), the archangel Raphael is mentioned.

• Gabriel (foundation) means "God is My Strength." In the three religions of "The Book" (Bible)—Judaism, Christianity, and Islam—he is one of the top two angels, along with Michael. He and Michael are the only two angels named directly in the Old Testament (other angels are secretly known but not named). Cayce's readings state, "Gabriel is, to be sure, the Announcer." (5277-1) Gabriel presides over Paradise and is the ruler of the First Heaven. Mohammed said Gabriel (Jibril, in Islam) dictated the Koran to him. Gabriel is the Guardian Angel of the Ismaelites (the Arabs). He is the angel who appeared to the prophet Daniel and told him all about the future of his people, and was the first to announce the coming of the Messiah. Legend holds that Gabriel was the man–angel that Jacob wrestled with to gain his blessing and new name, Israel. (Genesis 32:24)

• Metatron (kingdom) means the "lesser Yahweh," ruler of the first emanation, who also rules this tenth and final emanation. This is the *only* emanation that is able to contain God's initial expressive explosion of light, life, and consciousness. No other emanation could contain such power and intensity.

Other Angels

On occasion, another angel spoke through the "sleeping" Cayce. An angelic being named Halaliel (pronounced *Ha-la-lee-EL* or *Ha-la-leel*) first identified himself through the trance–state Cayce on October 15, 1933, during a Study Group reading on the lesson titled, "Day and Night," and spoke through Cayce off and on for about three years. There had been fifty–five readings given to this Study Group at that time. Occasionally, messages had come through the sleeping Cayce from other entities in the spirit realms, but never before was the complete reading credited to a single spirit entity. The reading began and continued as usual, but it ended on a strange note. Here is the last question of this reading and the answer given.

Q: Comment upon the following . . . does it carry any light of truth?

The Creator, in seeking to find or create a being worthy of companionship, realized that such a being would result only from a free will exercising its divine inheritance and through its own efforts find its Maker. Thus, to make the choice really a Divine one caused the existence of states of consciousness, that would indeed tax the free will of a soul; thus light and darkness. Truly, only those tried so as by fire can enter in.

A: The only variation that we would make is that all souls in the beginning were *one* with the Father. The separation, or turning away, brought evil. Then there became the necessity of the awareness of self's being out of accord with, or out of the realm of blessedness; and, as given of the Son, "yet learned he obedience through the things which he suffered."

COME, my children! Ye no doubt have gained from the comment this day, a new initiate has spoken in or through this channel; Halaliel [?], that was with those in the beginning who warred with those that separated themselves and became as naught.   262-56

The closing line is referring to the legendary battle between the angels of rebellion, led by Lucifer, and the angels of light, led by Michael. Apparently, Halaliel was among those angels of light that warred with the separating angels, who later became known as the Fallen Angels.

The next time Halaliel is mentioned by the sleeping Cayce is on October 24, 1933, at the morning reading. This time the reading is a "research reading" dealing with the subjects of psychic phenomena, spirit–ism, and spiritualism. The reading ends very strangely again, giving a list of entities who can be of help in gaining a better understanding of these concepts, instructing the conductor (Gertrude Cayce, Edgar's wife) to call upon these "forces" to be present for the next reading.

> The forces gathered here may be used in gaining this concept. As ye seek, ask first if all these are present: Lamech, Confucius, Tamah, Halaliel, Hebe, Ra, Ra-Ta, John.   5756-10

That very afternoon, at the 3 p.m. reading, Gertrude began the reading in accord with the morning suggestion.

> GC (Gertrude Cayce): If the "forces" Lamech, Confucius, Tamah, Halaliel, Hebe, Ra, Ra-Ta, John are present, we seek the answer to the following question.   5756-11

Gladys' notes at the end of this reading include this statement: "Edgar Cayce said on waking that he would like to always feel surrounded by as helpful influences as he did this time."

On January 7, 1934, the fifty–seventh Study Group reading was given, and one of those in attendance asked, "Who is Halaliel?" Here's the answer:

> One in and with whose courts Ariel fought when there was the rebellion in heaven. Now, where is heaven? Where is Ariel, and who was he? A companion of Lucifer or Satan, and one that made for the disputing of the influences in the experiences of Adam in the Garden.   262-57

Clearly, we are dealing with the legendary war of the angels. All of the angels were originally created in the image of the Creator, but through the misuse of free will, some rebelled against the cooperative spirit of Oneness. This rebellion would not be allowed; it was like a cancer in the Universal Consciousness. So, they were driven from heaven until such time that they repented of their self-seeking ways and re-attuned themselves to the Creator's harmonious spirit of oneness. Notice that the literal meanings of their names are quite beautiful and powerful, as they were originally intended to be: Ariel means "lion of God" and Lucifer means "light giver." The name Satan is actually from a Hebrew word that simply means "adversary." This is why the Messiah is often called the "advocate"; he is our counter influence to the adversary.

At the end of this reading, Gladys noted that Edgar Cayce had a slightly different experience during the reading. Normally, he would go to the Hall of Records to receive the Book of Life (the records) of the individual for whom the reading was being given. This time, however, he felt that a "group activity" took place in the back of the building where he received the records. Could this have been the group of La-mech, Confucius, Tamah, Halaliel, Hebe, Ra, Ra-Ta, and John?

The very next time Halaliel is mentioned is on the 8th of January, 1934, in a reading for a female society leader and Theosophist (443). She had been asking a series of very involved questions about mysticism and spiritual truth, then she asked:

Q: How high is this source that this information is being given from?
A: From the universal forces, and as emanated through the teacher that gives same—as one that has been given—Halaliel.   443-3

A few days later, on the 19th of January, we get the first earth changes material delivered by Halaliel, or at least some portion of the reading was from Halaliel, because he says so in the midst of the reading. This whole reading is unusual. For the first time, they are using a recording instrument to record the reading. Instead of Gertrude conducting, their eldest son, Hugh Lynn Cayce was the conductor; and in his opening suggestion to Edgar, he instructs Edgar to stop every fifteen minutes so the recording device can be reloaded. Amazingly, the sleeping Edgar stops exactly every fifteen minutes throughout the reading, even if he is in mid-sentence. Here is Hugh Lynn's opening suggestion and the sleeping Edgar's response:

HLC (Hugh Lynn Cayce): We seek at this time such information as will be of value and interest to those present . . . regarding the spiritual, mental and physical changes which are coming to the earth. You will tell us what part we may play in meeting and helping others to understand these changes. At the end of each fifteen minute period you will pause, until I tell you to continue, while the recording instrument is being arranged. You will speak distinctly at a normal rate of speech, and you will answer the questions which we ask.

EC (Edgar Cayce): Yes; as each of you gathered here have your own individual development, yet as each seeks to be a channel of blessings to the fellow man, each attunes self to the Throne of universal information. And, there may be accorded you that which may be beneficial, not only in thine own experience, but that which will prove helpful, hopeful, in the experience of others.

3976-15

From here, the reading goes into a brief description of the number and nature of the spirit entities that are gathered about them now to help with this reading. Then, the reading tells of the return of one of their members to the earth to help with this coming period of earth changes. The returning entity is the disciple John the Beloved, writing of the John's Gospel and the Revelation. Then the reading begins to address physical and mental changes, often referred to as "earth changes."

As to the material changes that are to be as an omen, as a sign to those that this is shortly to come to pass—as has been given of old, the sun will be darkened and the earth shall be broken up in divers places—and *then* shall be *proclaimed*—through the spiritual interception in the hearts and minds and souls of those that have sought His way—that *His* star has appeared, and will point the way for *those that enter into the holy of holies* in themselves. For, God the Father, God the Teacher, God the director, in the minds and hearts of men, must ever be in those that come to know Him as first and foremost in the seeking of those souls; for He is first the *God* to the individual and as He is exemplified, as He is manifested in the heart and in the acts of the body, of the individual, He becomes manifested before men. And those that seek in the latter portion of the year of our Lord (as ye have counted in and among men) '36, He will appear. (3976-15, my emphasis is italicized.)

My emphasis isolates the phrase that fits so well with the visions of the Prophet Daniel. Recall that one of Daniel's items was entering the sanctuary, the holy of holies within each of us. Here, Halaliel speaks to the same activity, saying that those who go within their sanctuary will know, will be guided. The "He will appear" phrase is developed further elsewhere in the Cayce readings, stating that the Messiah first comes in the hearts and minds of those who seek this influence, then it moves into the physical realm, ultimately becoming fully manifest, as we are, *incarnate*. Cayce says, "He will walk and talk with people of every clime." Here, Halaliel is stating that the beginning of this process is in "'36" (presumably, 1936), for those who seek within themselves. Interestingly, Cayce stated that Jesus Christ will return with the same body he took with him in Galilee (5749-4). Then, Halaliel continues, focusing on earth changes, and suddenly addresses the biblical prophecy of the Armageddon (Revelation 16:16):

As ye have seen those in lowly places raised to those of power in the political, in the machinery of nations' activities, so shall ye see those in high places reduced and calling on the waters of darkness to cover them. And those that in the inmost recesses of theirselves awaken to the spiritual truths that are to be given, and those places that have acted in the capacity of teachers among men, the rottenness of those that have ministered in places will be brought to light, and turmoils and strifes shall enter. And, as there is the wavering of those that would enter as emissaries, as teachers, from the throne of life, the throne of light, the throne of immortality, and wage war in the air with those of darkness, then know ye the Armageddon is at hand. For with the great numbers of the gathering of the hosts of those that have hindered and would make for man and his weaknesses stumbling blocks, they shall wage war with the spirits of light that come into the earth for this awakening; that have been and are being called by those of the sons of men into the service of the living God. For He, as ye have been told, is not the God of the dead, not the God of those that have forsaken Him, but those that love His coming, that love His associations among men—the God of the *living*, the God of Life! For, He *is* Life.   3976-15

At this point, the reading shifts back to the return of John the Beloved, whose name is stated as "John Peniel" (pronounced, *pen-ee-EL* or *pen-neal*). Of course, *peniel* means "face of God" in Hebrew, and was the name Jacob gave to the place where he met God face-to-face. Jacob's own name was changed to *Israel*, which means "strives with God." The reading says that John will be known in America by those that have gone through the regeneration in their bodies, minds, and spirits, and that he will give "the new order of things." John will be able to make these things "*plain* in the minds of men, that they may know the truth, the life, the light, will make them free." Then, the reading goes into an intense, inspiring call to awaken, filled with biblical phrases and ending with Halaliel identifying himself as the deliverer of this information:

I have declared this, that has been delivered unto me to give unto you, ye that sit here and that hear and that see a light breaking in the east, and have heard, have seen thine weaknesses and thine faultfindings, and know that He will make thy paths straight if ye will but live that ye know this day—then, may the next step, the next word, be declared unto thee. For ye in your weakness have known the way, through that as ye have made manifest of the Spirit of truth and light that has been proclaimed into this earth, that has been committed unto the keeping of Him that made of Himself no estate but who brought into being all that ye see manifest in the earth, and has declared this message unto thee: "Love the Lord thy God with all thine heart," and the second is like unto it, "Love thy neighbor as thyself." Who is thine neighbor? Him that ye may aid in whatsoever way that he, thy neighbor, thy brother, has been troubled. Help him to stand on his own feet. For such may only know the acceptable way. The weakling, the unsteady, must enter into the crucible and become as naught, even as He, that they may know the way. I, Halaliel, have spoken . . .

Q: Is there any further counsel or advice for us gathered here, which will enable us to understand better our responsibility?

A: All gathered here in the name of God who is the Father, to those that seek to know His ways—and who is as something outside the veil of their understanding unless sought, even as the counsel of the Father, of that God-Mother in each soul that seeks to know the biddings; not as one that would reap vengeance but rather as the loving, *merciful* Father. For, as ye show mercy, so may the Father show mercy to thee. As ye show the wisdom, as ye show the love of thy fellow man, so may the love be shown, so may the wisdom, so may the guiding steps day by day be shown thee. Be ye joyous in the Lord, knowing that He is ever present with those that seek His face. He is not in heaven, but makes heaven in thine own heart, if ye accept Him. He, God, the Father, is present and manifest in that ye mete to your fellow man in thine own experience.

Would ye know the Father, be the father to thy brother. Would ye know the love of the Father, show thy love to thy faltering, to thy erring brother—but to those that seek, not those that condemn.

We are through.   3976-15

Halaliel continues to make appearances in the readings over the next several months of 1934. On the 9th of September, the Study Group met again for its seventy–first reading, receiving what they believed to be further information about Halaliel, though it is not clearly stated as such in the reading. Here's what they heard and assumed to be referring to Halaliel:

To all we would give: Be patient. That part thou hast chosen in such a work is born of truth. Let it come in and be a part of thy daily life. Look in upon the experiences, for, as will be seen, my children, there has been appointed one that may aid thee in thy future lessons, and he will be thy teacher, thy guide, [Halaliel?] one sent through the power of thine own desires. Thine own selves, then, may present his being, meeting, living, dwelling, with thee. Not the Christ, but His messenger, with the Christ from the beginning, and is to other worlds what the Christ is to this earth.   262-71

Some in the Study Group, including Hugh Lynn Cayce, wanted to reject Halaliel's help, fearful that they might be led away from Christ. They ultimately did reject his help and asked that only the Christ guide them. Gladys notes that "two or three in the group were still not convinced that we were right in rejecting Halaliel's help in preparing the lessons." Whatever the truth about Halaliel, we hear nothing from him again, and his earth–changes comments are often questioned by those that feel he was not a high source, despite the reading's comments to the contrary. Fortunately, we have many other Cayce readings on earth changes that support and expand Halaliel's prophecies.

Another angel, or rather an archangel, occasionally spoke through the trance–state Cayce, usually when he and his little band of helpers were getting off track or fighting amongst themselves. It was Michael. Here are a few of those discourses:

Hark! There comes the voice of one who would speak to those gathered here: (pause)

I am Michael, lord of the Way! Bend thy head, oh ye children of men! Give heed unto the way as is set before you in that Sermon on the Mount, in that on yon hill this enlightenment may come among men; for even as the voice of the one who stood beside the sea and called all men unto the way, that those that would harken might know there was again a staff in David, and the rod of Jesse has not failed: for in Zion thy names are written, and in service will come truth! (254-42; italics are used to emphasize the loudness of Edgar's booming voice when Michael speaks.)

Here's another example:

Bow thine heads, ye children of men! For I, Michael, lord of the Way, would speak with thee! Ye generation of vipers, ye adulterous generation, be warned! There is today before thee good and evil! Choose thou whom ye will serve! Walk in the way of the Lord! Or else there will come that sudden reckoning, as ye have seen! Bow thine heads, ye who are ungracious, unrepentant! For the glory of the Lord is at hand! The opportunity is before thee! Accept or reject! But don't be *pigs!* Do keep the body in that manner of activity as to eliminate the poisons. And then keep the body-mind, the body-physical, clean in the sight of thy God.

294-208

Cayce was questioned about angels, archangels, and specifically the archangel Michael. Here are a few of his responses:

(Q) Are angels and archangels synonymous with that which we call the laws of the universe? If so, explain and give an example.
(A) They are as the laws of the universe; as is Michael, the lord of the Way, *not* the Way but the lord of the Way, hence disputed with the influence of evil as to the way of the spirit of the teacher or director in his entrance through the outer door. [See Jude 1:9 in re Michael the archangel "when contending with the devil about the body of Moses" when Moses died.]
(Q) You will give at this time a discourse on the subject, "Angels and Archangels, and How They Help Humanity."
(A) Yes. With the bringing into creation the manifested forms, there came that which has been, is, and ever will be, the spirit realm and its attributes—designated as angels and archangels. They are the spiritual manifestations in the spirit world of those attributes that the developing forces accredit to the One Source, that may be seen in material planes through the influences that may aid in development of the mental and spiritual forces through an experience—or in the acquiring of knowledge that may aid in the intercourse one with another.

5749-3

(Q) What is the relationship between Michael the lord of the way, and Christ the way?
(A) Michael is an archangel that stands before the throne of the Father. The Christ is the Son, the way *to* the Father, and one that came into the earth as man, the Son of man, that man might have the access to the Father; hence the way. Michael is the lord or the guard of the change that comes in every soul that seeks the way, even as in those periods when His manifestations came in the earth.

"Bow thine heads, O ye sons of men, would ye know the way: for

I, Michael, the lord of the Way, would warn thee that thou stand-est not in the way of thy brother nor sittest in the seats of the scornful, but rather make known that love, that glory, that power in his name, that none be afraid; for I, Michael, have spoken!"

[Stenographer's note: The above reading was so powerfully given that many of us were moved to tears; all were touched deeply.]

(262-28)

3

✦◈✦

Encounters with Angels

Biblical Encounters with Angels

There are 194 encounters with angels mentioned in the Bible, some by the spirit of a guiding angel, some are actual physical appearances of an angel, and some encounters with an angel occurred in dreams. A full fifty-three of these encounters occurred in the apostle John's visionary Revelation.

The first angelic appearance is to Hagar, the handmaiden of Sarah in Genesis 16:7. In fact, Hagar and her son Ishmael, by Abraham, experience *five* appearances of an angel of the Lord. Later in Genesis 22:11, when Abraham is about to sacrifice his son Isaac, by Sarah, an angel of the Lord appears and stops him. In Genesis 24, an angel of the Lord guides Abraham's highest-ranking servant in an assignment to find a wife for Abraham's son Isaac from among the kindred of Abraham back in the old country—he finds the now famous Rebecca, the eventual mother of Jacob, father of the twelve tribes of Israel. In Genesis

41

31:10, Jacob receives a message from an angel in a dream. One of the most famous angelic appearances was to Moses in Exodus 3:2, when an angel of the Lord appeared as a flame of fire in the midst of a bush that appeared to be on fire but did not burn. Here the angel teaches Moses how to raise the serpent off the desert floor and transform it into a magical staff to perform miracles before pharaoh. Much later Jesus refers Nicodemus to this event saying, "And as Moses lifted up the serpent in the wilderness, so must the Son of man be lifted up, that whoever believes in him may have eternal life." The mystery in this saying is that Nicodemus would have known that not only did Adam and Eve fall from grace in the Garden of Eden, but the serpent fell also. And the serpent represented the life force, the *élan vital*, or in Eastern terms, the *Kundalini*. And this energy is not only physical but also mental and emotional. In the Eastern teachings, these two qualities of energy are symbolized as wheels (chakras) and levels of awareness (lotuses). In order for Moses to perform miracles and to eventually come up on the mountain and meet God face-to-face, he had to raise the life force of his body and the consciousness of his mind, symbolized in the raising of the serpent off the desert floor. Later, when all the people are out in the desert with Moses, he has to do this again, because the people are poisoned by serpents—these are the "serpents" of lower vibrations and awareness. When Moses places a serpent on a raised staff, the suffering people are all healed by the image—because their deeper consciousness perceives the meaning of this image, this symbol: raise the life force within you to higher levels of vibration and awareness.

Throughout the Exodus, God sends an angel before them to protect and guide them to the Promised Land.

The Edgar Cayce readings add an interesting perspective to Jesus' use of the name *Israel*. Cayce says that the *real* Israel is reflected in the origin of this name, which is Jacob seeking so persistently to be blessed by God that he actually wrestles with an angel of God's until the angel finally agrees to bless him. Here's that passage. Notice that Jacob is "by himself" yet wrestling, this is the indication that he is in the Spirit wrestling with an angel of the Lord.

> Then Jacob was by himself; and a man was fighting with him till dawn.

But when the man saw that he was not able to overcome Jacob, he gave him a blow in the hollow part of his leg, so that his leg was damaged.

And he said to him, "Let me go now, for the dawn is near." But Jacob said, "I will not let you go till you have given me your blessing."

Then he said, "What is your name?" And he said, "Jacob."

And he said, "Your name will no longer be Jacob, but Israel: for in your fight with God and with men you have overcome."

Then Jacob said, "What is your name?" And he said, "What is my name to you?" Then he gave him a blessing.

And Jacob gave that place the name of Peniel, saying, I have seen God face to face, and still I am living. (Genesis 32:24-30 BBE)

Here's Cayce's explanation of this.

This is the meaning, this should be the understanding to all: Those that seek are Israel. Those that seek not, have ye not heard, "Think not to call thyselves the promise in Abraham. Know ye not that the Lord is able to raise up children of Abraham from the very stones?" So Abraham means *call;* so Israel means *those who seek.* How obtained the supplanter [the name *Jacob* in Hebrew means "supplanter"] the name Israel? For he wrestled with the angel, and he was face to face with seeking to know His way. So it is with us that are called and seek His face; we are the Israel. (262-28; my italics)

Israel is the seeker after truth.   5377-1

In the Bible, it is not unusual for an angel to be referred to as "a man." Here's an example from Zechariah:

"I saw in the night, and behold, a man riding upon a red horse! [This red horse is also found in the Revelation.] He was standing among the myrtle trees in the glen, and behind him were red, sorrel, and white horses. Then I said, 'What are these, my lord?' The angel who talked with me said to me, 'I will show you what they are.' So the man who was standing among the myrtle trees answered, 'These are they whom the Lord has sent to patrol the earth.' And they answered the angel of the Lord who was standing among the myrtle trees, 'We have patrolled the earth, and behold, all the earth remains at rest.' Then the angel of the Lord said, 'O Lord of hosts, how long will you have no mercy on Jerusalem and the cities of Judah, against which you have been angry these seventy years?' And the Lord answered gracious and comforting words to the angel who talked with me." (Zechariah 1:8-13, ESV)

And in the story of Abram and the three "men" that were on their way to Sodom and Gomorrah to judge it and destroy it if necessary, the men are actually angels. You may recall that Abram talked them into sparing the cities if they could find ten good people among the population—but they only found four, Lot, his wife, and two daughters.

A most interesting encounter with an angel occurs when Balaam, on a donkey, attempts to go along a path. The lowly donkey sees a fierce angel of the Lord standing in the path, but her master does not see it and keeps trying to force her forward on the path. Three times the donkey tries to avoid the angel; and three times Balaam whips her, until the donkey can't take it anymore and *speaks* to Balaam! This had to shock Balaam, and at that moment the angel makes his presence known to Balaam. Immediately Balaam falls to the ground and humbles himself before the angel and asks forgiveness for his sins. (Numbers 22:23–35)

In Judges 2:4, an angel of the Lord speaks to "all the people," breaking the pattern of speaking only to individuals.

In Judges 13:18, an angel explains to Manoah that an angel's name is secret. In post–biblical times, many of the secret names of angels have been published and used in magical spells and to evoke the angel's presence and power.

In II Samuel 24:16, the Lord stays the hand of His angel of destruction who was casting a plague among the people for their evil ways, saying, "It is enough." And the angel stops. This foreshadows the angels of destruction that are so active in the book of the Revelation. And though it appears to be vengeance, it is actually a cleansing, a purging of the earthy influences in the hearts and minds of the people, causing them to come away stronger and wiser about good and evil, light and dark, health and illness, and the like.

In the two books of Kings, Elijah has many experiences with "an angel of the Lord," including one who feeds him in the wilderness. In the book of Daniel, it is recorded that "an angel of the Lord" closed the mouths of the lions that were to eat Daniel in the lion's den.

Stories of angels and angel help are also found in the New Testament, particularly bringing messages of information and prophecy and even guiding incarnate people for their protection from evil people, such as Joseph's dream in which an angel warns him to flee for Herod is going to kill all male babies under two years of age in an effort to kill the prophesied "King of the Jews" that the three wise men from the East came to see. The angel specifically instructs Joseph to flee to Egypt, and then returns to Joseph after Herod's death, informing him that it is safe to return to Jerusalem.

As I stated in the beginning, the Revelation has fifty-three encounters with angels, even one in which the archangel Michael comes into John's vision. Here's that passage:

> "Now war arose in heaven, Michael and his angels fighting against the dragon. And the dragon and his angels fought back, but he was defeated and there was no longer any place for them in heaven. And the great dragon was thrown down, that ancient serpent, who is called the Devil and Satan, the deceiver of the whole world—he was thrown down to the earth, and his angels were thrown down with him." (Revelation 12:7-9, ESV)

This passage indicates that Satan and his fallen angels are in the Earth! This would explain some of the fear that captured the hearts and minds of many, and the centuries of purging people deemed to be possessed by the evil forces of Satan and his angels, such as the cruel Inquisition and hysterical witch trials. As was revealed in the Cayce discourses and in the previous chapter of this book, there is indeed evil, and it can and does possess people. Cayce was asked about the anti-Christ in this reading:

> "(Q) In what form does the anti-Christ come, spoken of in Revelation?

"(A) In the spirit of that opposed to the spirit of truth. The fruits of the spirit of the Christ are love, joy, obedience, long-suffering, brotherly love, kindness. Against such there is no law. The spirit of hate, the anti-Christ, is contention strife, fault-finding, lovers of self, lovers of praise. Those are the anti-Christ, and take possession of groups, masses, and show themselves even in the lives of men."   281-16

Clearly Cayce saw the anti–Christ as an evil *spirit* that takes possession of individuals, communities, nations, and the masses. This spirit has many of the same weaknesses of human nature: hate, contention with others and self, fault–finding in others and self, and egotistical qualities of self–exaltation and self–gratification. In some ways, this evil is more dangerous than evil beings, because most all humans have at one time or another experienced these attitudes, emotions, and dispositions. I've actually known them personally to come and go within me and those I share life with! And when I read about the serpent in the Garden of Eden (and archangel Michael identifies the Revelation's red dragon as originally being that serpent) and how it deceived Eve, it strikes me that this could have been a "spirit" within Eve's heart and mind rather than an entity outside of her. She could have rationalized how the forbidden fruit was not actually as deadly as stated. Rationalizing conduct is another common human tendency. This brings us to God's attempt to keep Cain from killing his brother: "The Lord said to Cain, 'Why are you angry, and why has your face fallen? If you do well, will you not be accepted? And if you do not do well, sin is couching at the door. Its desire is for you, but you must rule it.'" (Genesis 4:6–7). The sin is "couching" at the door of Cain's heart and mind. We all may carry the potential for the spirit of the anti–Christ to take hold of us, and each of us must gain control over this.

In the very last chapters of the Bible and the Revelation, it is written that the "Alpha and Omega, the beginning and the end" has sent his angels to us many times to teach, protect, and guide us.

Personal Encounters with Angels

A longtime A.R.E. member and volunteer shared her important protective encounter with an angel, likely her guardian angel. Here's her story as she shared it with me and allowed me to share it with you.

> "I met a man at an A.R.E. event. We hit it off. He was fun and smart. We didn't live near each other, so our activities included taking trips together. On the second trip, I was waiting for him to take a shower so we could be on our way. Suddenly, a very strong, ten-foot tall, masculine angel stood before me, with his arms folded over his chest. He seemed to be glaring at me and then dipped his head in the direction of my friend. I got that I was not to get any more involved with this friend. Several months later that same year, the now ex-friend got married. She was his fourth wife. On one occasion, they had a heated argument and he ended up shooting her. He has been in prison ever since. The angel was wearing a long, white robe and seemed to emanate light. He just appeared out of nowhere. When you meet an angel, you have no doubts!"

I'll share one of my experiences with an angel, and very much a "guardian angel."

It was forty-some years ago, and I was in my mid-twenties and traveling from North Dakota into South Dakota by myself in my car in the wee hours of the morning, say one to two a.m. in the morning. It was very dark. I was the only car on the road. This is where the Bad Lands to the north and the grassy prairies to the south meet. As I entered South Dakota and was heading across the northern part of the state, intending to turn south and head into Nebraska, I saw a hitchhiker dimly lit by my headlights. Now normally I'd be out of my right mind to pull over and pick this guy up out there at that hour, but something in me was turning the wheel to pull off the road and allow him in my car. As I pulled back onto the road, he asked me where I was going. I told him that I was going to a numbered route (don't remember the number today) and turning south heading to Nebraska. He then told me not to take that road because the natives on the Pine Ridge Indian Reservation had shot some FBI agents and some of them may take a shot at a white boy driving through their territory. At this time in my life, I was not reading newspapers or watching TV news, so I hadn't heard anything about this. The hitchhiker told me to go up to another road beyond the reservation and to make my southerly turn there. He also told me that I could let him out when I made that turn. As I made the turn, I pulled off the road and let him out. I turned to see if the road was clear for me to pull back onto it and then turned back to be sure he was out of the way of my car. But he was nowhere to be seen. I looked all around. I even got out of the car and looked for him. Now this area was flat to the horizon. You could see forever. But this man was nowhere to be seen. He simply disappeared. Then the hair on the back of my neck rose up, and I became alarmed and slightly frightened. My body had a tingling vibration of excitement. I quickly realized that I had just given a ride to an angel that appeared as a man, and that this angel was sent to keep me from upsetting some people who were already angry, and directing their anger toward me. I got back into my car and sat there for a while, breathing heavily and reflecting on how the unseen world had connected with me that night for my sake. I said a few prayers before starting back on my trip. All the way to Nebraska the experience circled around my mind. I kept seeing him standing in my headlights in the darkness with his thumb out and the pull I felt toward him. I kept hearing his voice, how calm it was and how matter-of-fact. He made no small talk and showed no emotion, but was pleasant. I realized that I never felt any fear of him while in my car alone on that deserted highway in the dark. Even today as I write this I get excited and tingly by the telling of it.

Next we have experience from another A.R.E. friend and volunteer. She is not sure that her experience was with an angel, but it certainly was a being like an angel.

"When I was a very young child, I was often visited in the middle of the night by a very old-looking man with a long white beard dressed in white robes. He was surrounded with a soft white light and even seemed to be *made* of this light because I could see *through* him but never really thought it strange, nor was I ever frightened of him. He would sit near by my bed rocking in a rocking chair (which also seemed made of the same transparent light) and read to me from a very thick and ancient-looking book. There were no chairs in my room and all my books were the 'little golden' types. There was a vague feeling of familiarity, as though I somehow knew him from somewhere, and his presence was comforting. The stories he read me seemed to have something to do with distant times and experiences that I had no memory of, but all I could ever remember in the morning was that he had been there. I know these were not dreams, though you may find that hard to believe. To this day, sixty years later, I still wonder who and what he was, and often wish he would come to me again."

Here's the experience of an exhausted young mother whose deceased mother came to help her and her sleepless child. Her mother had passed on when she was four weeks pregnant with this child.

"I was completely exhausted and yet my baby would not go to sleep. I paced the hall with her in the stroller until I got to a breaking point. Then I prayed to Mary, the mother of Jesus, and to my mother to help me. The baby fell asleep, as did I. But in my dream I saw my deceased mother come to us and begin playing with my baby, in the very hall we had just been pacing, tossing her up in the air and laughing. I said, 'What are you doing! I need her to sleep!' My mother replied that she was wearing her out for me, so I could rest. Then, as I watched Mom in my dream, she began to grow larger and larger, and huge wings like an angel's wings appeared on her back. I was shocked, and said, 'Mom? You're growing!' She simply smiled back at me, as to confirm that this was okay and she was an angel. Her wings were thick and she filled the doorway with her size. She glowed with an incredible white light. She radiated happiness and confidence."

In the Cayce teachings, we are all angels at a higher level of expression than our current physical condition, and we all may act as helping or guiding or even guardian angels. One of his most interesting examples of humans being angels is in his discourses on the biblical

Revelation. Scholars consider the author of the Revelation to have been the apostle John (Rev. 1:1, 1:9; 21:2, 22:8), who also wrote the Gospel and three Epistles. John and Peter taught and helped the new community. (Acts 3) The Romans arrested both of them, and Paul. They were tried and convicted of activities subversive to the authority of the land, the Romans. Peter and Paul were sentenced to death but John, captured in Ephesus, was ordered banished to the island of Patmos in the Aegean Sea. And that is where he was when he experienced the Revelation and wrote it down. According to Edgar Cayce, before Peter and John separated, Peter promised John that he would endeavor to come to him after the Romans put him to death, and to communicate with him from heaven. According to Cayce, it is the deceased Peter in angelic spirit who later appears to John twice during his vision or revelation. So glorious is Peter's form as the angel that John falls down to worship it as a heavenly expression of God (Rev. 19:10 and 22:8–9). But, in these two appearances, the angel clearly identifies himself as one of John's *brethren*, saying, "You must not do that! I am a fellow servant with you and with your brethren." Cayce explains (281–16) that the deceased Peter was this angel—it was Peter in the higher, superconscious state of being, and as such, he appeared to John as an angelic expression of God. Recall that a portion of us was initially made in the image of God in Genesis 1:26. Even Jesus stated that we are gods, and referred us to Psalm 82:6: "You are gods; and all of you are children of the Most High."

In the Cayce teachings, we are all angels at a higher level of our multilevel being, and we all act as helping or guiding or even guardian angels at times when not incarnate. However, I have received stories in which the person acted as an angel while they were definitely still incarnate, and one of those follows:

In this next encounter, a lady acts as an angel at times and also encounters angels, flying with them.

"People have seen me as an angel, they say that I appear to them with large white wings, etc., and they know it's me. I believe that we are all angels, doing our work with each other. Most of us are just not conscious of it. I don't recall being in angel form, as the people have seen me, though I've appeared to some when they were in great fear. I calmed them down. Don't recall that myself; they call and tell me that I appeared to them. Though one time, I was at work, and I had this sudden urge to meditate. I sat down and meditated for a few minutes, then got up and went back to work. It was at that time that a friend said I appeared to him in a frightening situation and calmed him down. On another occasion, I was in a meditation and suddenly found myself flying between two angels, wings and all. We were flying over Washington State, as I was deciding whether to move back to that area or not and was living on the East Coast at the time. I now live in the Pacific Northwest."

Here's another encounter with an angel:

"In 1974, I had very difficult but successful surgery on my right kidney. Late that night, I became aware that I was in agony from the pain. The worse part was that I couldn't move or shift my position in bed. I couldn't even reach the few inches to touch the nurse's call button. I thought if only I could shift my body to a more comfortable position I could relieve some of the pain and call a nurse. The light in the room was low. As I was praying for help, a man came into the room dressed in scrubs saying he was a nurse and here to help. He lifted me and rearranged me in bed, which helped greatly. I was so grateful! He said something that made me laugh a little and then left. When I asked the nursing staff about him the next day they looked perplexed. They didn't have a male nurse on staff. It was quickly attributed to the effects of the medications. *I know it was an angel.* Throughout my life I have often been aware of their presence and dearly love them."

Here's another:

"When I was three years old, I was in bed experiencing extreme fear because of the violence of my parents. I looked to the foot of my bed and saw a glowing being the size of an adult. Its presence completely relieved me of my fear. I knew that I was loved and my love and faith was felt or known beyond my childhood environment. This light being appeared at other times when I so needed its reassurance."

Here's the story of a mother who found herself alone and caring for her child.

"I had just gotten divorced and moved across the country. Suddenly I was raising my three-year-old daughter on my own in a big city, trying to get back into the job market, and struggling to make ends meet. Scared, lonely, and depressed, I felt ill-prepared for the challenges I faced. Then one night I dreamed that a radiant woman with golden wings was sitting beside me on my bed, singing to me. She sang the same eight tones over and over to me in the same sequence. As she sang, she told me telepathically that those eight notes represented my name in the angelic realm and that it was important for me to remember them. (I'll never forget them.) Her voice was clear and sweet and beautiful. When I opened my eyes, the last note she sang was still reverberating in the air, and she was still sitting there beside me for one brief moment, smiling.

"That angelic encounter brought me hope and improved my confidence. When I started to worry, I would remind myself: 'My name is a beautiful song in the angelic realm; an angel came to tell me personally.' Knowing the angels cared about me seemed to open a communication channel in my mind. I started listening for angelic guidance and hearing it. It wasn't exactly like hearing a voice speaking—words and images would just pop into my head. Knowing that God's divine messengers were with me helped me endure all the turmoil and stress of that time. I stopped living in fear of the future. Relying on angelic support has improved the quality of my life immeasurably since that dark time several years ago. The angels have guided me about such mundane things as changing lanes to avoid traffic tie-ups. But they've also guided me in making important life decisions like applying for a better job and buying a new house. Now every morning when I wake up, I ask the angels, 'What do I need to know today?' And they give me helpful guidance for the day ahead. I record their messages in my journal. Then I say, 'Thank you, angels. I'm grateful for this day.

Please guide me through it.' And they always do."

And another encounter that was reported to me as follows:

"I had an unforgettable angel experience around my eighteenth birthday. It was a dream, and I think a very important one. Not long prior to the dream, my mother, sister, and I attended a community church service. There was an altar call—kind of a Billy Graham type appeal—that I felt a sudden urge to answer (as did a lot of the congregation). Mother and my sister followed me. At this time in my life, I had not spent any time pondering over what I believed. I had high ideals but at the same time, I was a silly teenager."

THE DREAM:

"I was in a lovely moonlit garden standing before a white gate. Suddenly, two angels appeared beside me. They were huge–bigger than life—and in full angelic regalia. I was awestruck and a little bit afraid. They asked me if I wanted to be baptized. I said, "Yes," but somewhat with fear and trembling. They opened the gate and led me to a round, deep pond. (In retrospect, it reminds me of the cenotes in the Mayan culture.) They told me to get into the water. I protested saying that I didn't swim very well and was afraid I'd drown. They assured me that they would be watching me so I trusted them and went into the pool.

"As soon as I entered the pool, the waters started swirling around like a whirlpool. It kept whirling faster and faster, and I was being sucked down and was fighting with all my might. I looked up at the angels and they just looked expressionless and watched me but made no move to help. The pond seemed like a large, deep well. Finally I was so exhausted that I decided I was going to drown and was about to give up fighting.

"I looked up one last time and saw Jesus, wearing a white robe. He reached down toward me with his right hand, and I reached up with my right hand, and I was out of the water instantly. I sat on a rock cliff beside Jesus, and he talked with me and I felt very loved. I wish I could remember what he said. I cannot but will never, ever forget the experience.

"Note: In trying to interpret this dream—part of which is obvious as it is telling me to look to and trust Jesus—I've always questioned those deceptive angels. Maybe their message and purpose was only to get me to Jesus and not follow other paths?

"I felt like I was going around in a wonderful glow for a while after that dream, but I didn't dare tell it to anyone. I was afraid it was some kind of calling to ministry or something. Of course, women were not ministers back then and all I could think of was missionary, which I knew little about, but my reaction was 'No.' So I suppressed the dream. I say suppressed, not repressed, because I couldn't forget it, but just didn't think about it anymore. Years later, in 1968, I prayed for God to show me the truth, and I'd follow it. And guess what! About six weeks after that prayer, I read Edgar Cayce's biography, *There Is a River*, and the dream came back into my full awareness! When I read the Philosophy chapter in his biography, I knew almost instantly that it was the answer to my prayer."

One of the many fascinating stories in the Edgar Cayce chronicles is about an incarnate woman who once was the guardian angel of one of Jesus' disciples! The story begins with Edgar and his wife Gertrude in Dayton, Ohio, giving a health reading for a man. In the course of giving the reading, the information comes through that the man's illness is due to his soul's activities in a past incarnation! This is the first time reincarnation appears in the Cayce readings. Edgar and Gertrude decide to get past life readings on each member of their family. Among their past lives, each was told they lived during the incarnation of Jesus Christ, except for Gertrude. This upsets her so much that they decide to get a follow-up to explain why Gertrude was not incarnate during Jesus's time since she loves Jesus just as much as anyone else in the family. The reading began by explaining that the directions given to the trance-state Edgar were for him to list incarnations, and Gertrude's soul was not *incarnate* at that time, because she was the guardian angel of the disciple Andrew! (538-59) The reading further stated that he would have fallen off of his righteous path often if she hadn't been there to help him. Well, as you can imagine, Gertrude was very happy to hear this!

4

◈

Fairies, Sprites, Elves, and More

ne of the most surprising readings Edgar Cayce gave was to an oilman seeking help finding a new oil field. The man asked if he should seek the help of a person in New York City or another in London, to which Cayce replied, "Rather had the entity best listen to the voices *from within,* that present themselves as the activities about the entity—or *brownies."* (1265-2) Brownies? Yes, brownies! This had to be a shock to those listening to this instruction. In fact, they weren't sure if they understood him correctly, so they followed up with another reading the next day, asking: "What is meant by the term 'brownies' in the last answer of the Check Reading?" The sleeping Cayce replied, "The manner in which those of the elementals—entities who have not entered into materiality—have manifested and do at times manifest themselves to the entity. Apparently this man was being approached by brownies but was not listening to them! Cayce went on to explain, "Brownies, pixies, fairies, gnomes are not elementals, but elements that are as definite *entities* as man materialized, see?" (1265-3) Here we see

Cayce parsing the details of elementals and entities, clarifying that fairies are of the elements but are in fact individuated entities like humans are as well. We'll have more on the elementals in Chapter 9. For now, we're focusing on the fairies and their variations, as well as other types of invisible little people.

To a young lady getting a reading, he said, "Don't be afraid to acknowledge that you see fairies as ye study, for you will nurture these experiences. Don't be afraid to say that you see the gnomes which would hinder peoples at times." (5359-1)

To another person getting a past-life reading, he explained, "Before this [incarnation] the entity was in the Scotch land. The entity began its activity as a prodigy, as one already versed in its associations with the unseen—or the elemental forces; the fairies and those of every form that do not give expression in a material way and are only seen by those who are attuned to the infinite." (2547-1)

A fascinating reading came when Cayce was asked how to put forth an argument to persuade a man to accept the deal that was being offered to him. Cayce explained that there were unseen forces preparing "proper connections and a proper set-up" that would ultimately affect the desired outcome, and if they were patient "the little brownies come along and tell him what to do!" (257-87)

Fairies, elves, and gnomes are beings affecting the world but remain mostly unseen. Brownies are actually of the family of fairies. Nymphs are female elves. Sprites are fairies of a particularly pleasant appearance and disposition. Pixies are mischievous fairies. Folklore describes them all as magical beings of diminutive human form. Gnomes are usually described as shriveled little old men that inhabit the interior of the Earth and act as guardians of its treasures.

It would seem that the young people today are closely "attuned to the infinite," as Cayce put it, and are therefore interested in books and movies about the normally unseen fairies, elves, and gnomes. Let's keep our eyes open, or as Jesus might have put it, whoever has eyes to see, let them see!

Unusual Beings in Legend and Lore

Let's now explore the lore and legends of all the unusual beings that are often listed among the mystical little people. The list would look something like this: fairies, pixies, sprites, brownies, nixies, gnomes, nature spirits, kobolds, duendes, goblins, wee folk, elves, fauns, trolls, the Fates (*Moirai*, pronounced either moi–*ruh* or *moy-rye*), and so on.

Though certainly among ancient lore and legend are mermaids, mermen, centaurs, satyrs, sirens, harpies, and others of these kinds, they are *not* fairies and are not among the mystical beings. They are monstrosities that predominantly lived in the physical world among humans, like the Nephilim in Genesis 6. They are the result of the wayward sons of God breeding with animals! Many consider them to be the Fallen Angels branch of the sons of God. In fact, implied in their name is "fallen," from the Hebrew root n-ph-l. (There were no vowels in Hebrew, but for us to pronounce these words, vowels were added.) Even though some writers attempt to connect fairies to the Nephilim, there is no connection that can be truly made. The Nephilim are clearly the uncontrollable giants: "There were giants in the earth in those days; and also after that, when the sons of God came in unto the daughters of men, and they bare children to them, the same became mighty men which were of old, men of renown." (Genesis 6:4) The word "renown" originally had a negative meaning something akin to "infamous," though today that connotation is lost. In the biblical book of Numbers 13:32–33, we find this account of the Nephilim: " . . . and all the people that we saw in it are of great height . . . the Nephilim (the sons of Anak, who come from the Nephilim), and we seemed to ourselves like grasshoppers, and so we seemed to them." A pre–Inca oral legend carried on by the Quechua natives of Peru tells of an unexpected landing of a remnant group of Nephilim on the shores of their lands. This legend describes the Nephilim as so gigantic that a good–size native warrior only stood as tall as the kneecap of a Nephil! This caused the people to move high up into the mountains. The legend says that these Nephilim were struggling to survive. They had no women among them and were hated by everyone. According to this ancient tale, the great Creator God cleanses the pre–Incan lands of these remnant giants in one single disastrous flood.

The Fates (the *Moirai*)

In Greek mythology, the *Moirai*, often known in English as "the Fates," were the three white-robed incarnations of Destiny. They were "Spinner" (*Clotho*), "Allotter" (*Lachesis*), and "Unturnable" (*Atropos*). They controlled the thread of life of every mortal from birth to death. They were independent and impersonal. They watched that the fate assigned to every being by eternal laws might take its course without obstruction. These views of fate imply that somehow time and space are not sequential but the past and the future exist at the same time. Thus, the future is known now and the past is still alive. Cayce's readings appear to support this idea when viewed from a higher level of perception: "Time is as one time, Space as one space, to the cosmic consciousness." (900-345) In ancient Indian philosophy we find a similar concept: "If all future occurrences are rigidly determined . . . coming events may in some sense be said to exist already. The future exists in the present, and both exist in the past. Time is thus on ultimate analysis *illusory*." (Arthur Llewellyn Basham, *History and Doctrines of the Ājīvikas*, (1951, p. 236)

I was chatting with a graduate of Atlantic University (founded by Cayce in 1930), who shared his belief that free will is only exercised in how we *respond* to the fated events of our lives, free will does not shape our lives or determine our lives. My own 95-year-old father has the same belief, sharing how he survived the three-hour-long attack on Pearl Harbor while his closest friend did not: "It simply wasn't my time." He believes that events in our lives, and especially the time of death, are predetermined; they are fated. One vivid scene in his memory is of him helping several men during the attack when an officer ordered him to leave that job and get the codes ashore. As he walked away from the men, a bomb hit them, killing everyone. That event and the image of those dead men, of whom he should have been one, solidified his fatalistic view of life. And consider Edgar Cayce's teaching that the prophecy recorded in the Great Pyramid in Egypt contains details about our yet-to-be-lived journey: "As recorded in the pyramid . . . there are periods when even the hour, day, year, place, country, nation, town, and individuals are pointed out." (5748-5) Even Jesus foretells his fate to be arrested and crucified in Jerusalem. More shocking is that the archangel Gabriel foretells Jesus' fate to the prophet Daniel, roughly 600 years before Jesus' birth! How can this be? Is it all known beforehand? Are we simply to live it, reacting as best we can? Are all events in our lives predetermined and therefore inevitable? Is the final judgment based on how well we handle our destiny? "Curiouser and curiouser!" Cried Alice in Wonderland.

Fairies

Fairies are not angels, fallen angels, dead humans, or beastly off-spring of ancient creatures. Surprisingly, and unlike angel lore, fairy lore never described them as having wings. That was a modern invention, likely in a semi-scientific attempt to explain how they could fly since magic was no longer an acceptable explanation. The idea of fairies having butterfly or dragonfly wings came during the Victorian Era from 1837 to 1901. Prior to this, it was believed that fairies flew via magic. Some fairies used enchanted ragwort stems, like the enchanted brooms of witches; some even flew on the backs of birds like humans ride on the backs of horses. But some, like the Lady of the Lake and others, simply used their magic to fly. And they could fly while carrying the dead weight of a full-grown man, like the wounded King Arthur.

Fairies come in many sizes and interests. They live in a realm that is just a thin veil away from the human world and usual stay near the life forces in Nature. You may have noticed that Edgar Cayce's childhood experiences with fairies were always around Nature. They may live in fairy communities or alone. They can be mischievous or magically helpful. Though in human form, they can be a half-inch tall or the full size of an adult human.

A classic view of fairies is that they are beings living just below angels and just above humans. However, during the early centuries of Christianity, and particularly during the Protestant Reformation, they were feared as being pagan and of the Devil. Many of these fears generated accusations that they were the Fallen Angels or the spirits of dead people. But when one looks at the unbiased legends and lore related to fairies, they were not associated with angels or discarnate spirits, but were a uniquely different species. They could breed with humans, and possibly with angels—as legend holds that the angels bred with humans in the aforementioned Genesis 6: "When men began to multiply on the surface of the ground, and daughters were born to them, God's sons [angelic beings] saw that men's daughters were beautiful, and they took any that they wanted for themselves as wives." (Genesis 6:1–2, WEB) There are many tales of humans with fairy wives and half–fairy–blood children born to them.

From Medieval times through the Reformation, terrible events were most often blamed on the Devil and his dark angels, or Lilith (meaning "night creature") of Hebrew legends. Such was the case for fairies too. If a baby was born with a deformity or abnormality, or developed one in infancy, it was blamed on fairy "changelings," a poor facsimile left behind when the true human baby was taken by the heartless, pagan fairies. There is much more on Lilith in the chapter on demons and dark Angels (withhold your judgment on Lilith until you read her whole story).

It is difficult to identify the origin of fairies; even the name's origin is a bit uncertain. Many researchers believe that the name originated with the Roman *Tria Fata*, the "Three Fates." We find this in the name, *Fata Morgana*, which is the Italian name for *Morgan le Fay*, the famous enchantress and half–sister of King Arthur (from the French *la fée*, meaning *fairy*). Fairies are often considered to be enchantresses, by virtue of their magical beauty, music, and song. Morgan le Fay may have also been the goddess *Morganis* who transported King Arthur to Avalon to heal him.

If fairies are truly related to the Fates, then their origin may be traced back to the Creation! In the earliest moments of the Great Creation, Egyptian legend tells how Ra conceived Ma'at, the goddess of justice. She weighed every heart in order to determine their fate. If the fairies did indeed originate among the Fates, then they have moved a long way from there to where they have been in recent millennia. They are now considered to be only an *occasional* influence in human lives, certainly not the forces of the Fates that they once were.

Shakespearean Fairies

In Shakespeare's works, we find these now famous fairies: Oberon and Titania, king and queen of the fairies in *A Midsummer Night's Dream* and again in Goethe's *Faust II*. Also in *A Midsummer Night's Dream* is Puck, the "shrewd and knavish sprite" who is a jester to Oberon. Ariel is the fairy spirit in *The Tempest*, and was freed by the magician Prospero from his imprisonment by the evil witch Sycorax (pronounced *sick-or-axe*).

A rather famous fairy makes her way into Shakespeare's *Romeo and Juliet*; she is Queen Mab, the "midwife of the fairies." In her more metaphysical role, she is the fairy who induces sleepers to dream, and as such she is the title of a chapter in *Moby Dick*, when Stubb dreams a dream in which a merman warns Stubb of the futility of fighting against Captain Ahab. Chaucer calls her Mabily. In the HBO series *True Blood*, the character Mab is the "Queen of the Fairies."

Tinker Bell & Periwinkle

In our time, the most famous fairy of all, especially for children, is Tinker Bell. Though Tinker Bell is a fictional character, first introduced by J.M. Barrie in his play *Peter Pan* in 1904, and later in the novel *Peter and Wendy* in 1911, Barrie truly understood fairies and gave Tinker Bell many of the characteristics of a true fairy. She is a mender of pots and pans, known as a "tinker," and her speech is like the sound of a tinkling bell, thus her name, Tinker Bell. Due to her small size, she can only experience one emotion at a time, and therefore cannot counterbalance her emotions, making her extreme in her feelings. In Barrie's play, she becomes ill tempered, jealous, and vindictive, as well as kind and helpful to Peter. Barrie teaches that humans can fly with the help of fairy dust (what Disney later called pixie dust).

Disney recently introduced Periwinkle as Tinker Bell's older sister, but she was quite a different fairy long before Disney got ahold of her. In 1906, Lily Grant Duff built her novel *Periwinkle* around this fairy, telling of how she appeared to be a human woman and interacted with human men, but was in fact a fairy from Fairyland.

Fairy Godmother & Fairy Guides

A *fairy godmother* is a magical spirit who guides a human as if their godparent. Countess Marie-Catherine d'Aulnoy (pronounced *dune-wah*—yes, I couldn't believe it either), a French writer who coined the term "fairy tale" (*contes des fées*) and wrote twenty-three fairy tales, was the first to conceive of the idea of a "fairy godmother." Again we find this idea goes all the way back to the feminine Fates, who guide and influence people's lives. It also has a root in the spiritual influence of dead mothers who help the youngsters in their still–incarnate families. Benefactors and protégées were common methods of learning and providing assistance through the Renaissance, and such ideas found their way into the idea of a fairy godmother. But helping humans was not the traditional interests and roles of fairies, for they mostly focused on their own lives and interests, and only occasionally interacted with humans. Traditionally, fairies did not seek to interfere in human lives. Yet, the lore does contain a few close ties between fairies and humans, even some marriages and half–fairy–blood children.

Akin to fairy godmother are *fairy guides*. Even Cayce mentions that God sometimes sends fairy guides. (338–3) He told a seven–year–old girl that in a previous incarnation in ancient Egypt she was " . . . the fairy to many of those in that period, for the entity lent aid in many a lowly place, as well as in the high; bringing peace and understanding . . . " And her name then was *Peri*, as in *Periwinkle*. (1911–1)

In the tale of *Sleeping Beauty*, Flora, Fauna, and Merriweather are fairy guardians sent to watch over mortals throughout their lives. In Carlo Collodi's 1883 book *The Adventures of Pinocchio*, there appears "the fairy with turquoise hair" (Italian, *La Fata dai Capelli Turchini*), who acts as a fairy guide to the wooden boy who wants to become a real boy. She appears along Pinocchio's journeys to warn the puppet boy against dangerous behavior. Although Pinocchio initially ignores her good advice and is attracted to all of the wild wonders of freedom, he later comes to fol-low her instruction after suffering much from his mistakes. In turn, she protects him, and enables him to transform into a real human boy. It was Disney who gave her the name of The Blue Fairy when adapting the story for the film *Pinocchio*. By not giving her a name but simply a description, Collodi was following a tradition of not saying the name of a fairy.

The Lady of the Lake

Among the legends of the fairies is the Lady of the Lake, a very magical fairy associate with Lancelot and the sword Excalibur. Among the oldest existing texts about Lancelot and the Lady of the Lake is a German work titled, *Lanzelet,* by Ulrich von Zatzikhoven, dating to the 1100s. According to this text, after the death of his father, Lancelot is taken by a fairy into her "island in the sea" when he was only a year old. At the age of fifteen he emerges from the lake to begin his knightly journeys as an "enchanted" nobleman. Here is a passage that gives us a glimpse into an underwater Fairyland:

> "A lady bore the child away, a wise fairy of the sea, a queen bet-ter than any in all the world to-day. In her realm she had ten thousand maidens, whereof none knew man or man's array. They wore shifts and kirtles [a sleeved, knee-length body garment] of samite [a heavy silk with threads of gold and silver] and of silk. I will not deny it, but I say not that it is sooth [truth], the Lady's land bloomed throughout the year as [if] it was mid-May, and her domain was fair and broad and long, and full of joy were its borders. The mountain whereon the mighty castle stood was of crystal, round as a ball. No stranger guest and no king's host was feared therein. All round about it lay the sea and a wall so strong that never a man might be bold enough to deem that he could avail aught against it, and albeit there was a gate, it was of hard-est adamant [a legendary rock]. There within they bided, knowing no fear. He that wrought the castle adorned it cunningly. Without and within it was of gold, like a star. Within its moat naught grew old, or even after a hundred years was less fair." (*The Fairies in Tradition and Literature*; Briggs, Katherine; Routledge & Kegan Paul, Lt. 1967, pages 5 and 6)

In the legends of the magician Merlin, he becomes infatuated with the wondrous Lady of the Lake, and is trapped by her for a time. Dur-ing his time with her, she learns all of his magical spells and powers. Curiously, Merlin foresaw this in a vision but did not resist the com-ing situation with her, even though it cost him dearly. She has various names but most common is Nimue (pronounced *nee-moo*) and Viviane (pronounced *viv-ee-ann*). She is also the enchantress who retrieves the magic sword Excalibur from the lake for King Arthur. She is considered to be the ruler of the Isle of Avalon. In 1190, Glastonbury Tor became the location of Avalon, meaning it was an island hill surrounded by a marsh (back then, the marsh is no longer there). The Lady of the Lake may also be one of the eight sisters of Morgan le Fay. And like Morganis, Nimue is a powerful healer. In some tales it is said that not just Morganis carried Arthur's mortally wounded body to Avalon to heal it, but *four* enchantresses carried him; Nimue may have been one of them.

Elves

Elves were clearly a different species than fairies up until the Elizabethan Era (1558–1603) when they were mixed together indiscriminately. Prior to this era, elves were clearly not fairies. In fact, elves were always more serious than fairies. Elves had burdens to carry and responsibilities to tend to, while fairies mostly lived with light hearts, music, dancing, and a carefree nature—that is until they came into contact with humans and their many problems and troubles.

Elves have pointed ears. Elves have human weaknesses more than fairies. And in the case of fairies, their failings are due more to loving naively, whereas elves have urges and seek to satisfy them by any means necessary. Much of the older elven lore and legend reveals especially strong libidos in elven men, even to the point of seeking out human women for sex. Fairies have no such legends.

Elven lore has deep roots in Old Norse and Germanic mythology, and there is a prayer book mentioning elves that dates back to sometime around 900 AD. (Hall, Alaric; *Elves in Anglo-Saxon England: Matters of Belief, Health, Gender and Identity* [Boydell Press, 2007; pp. 71–72]) The famous Old Norse *Poetic Edda* was written and published in the 1200s and preserved in Icelandic manuscripts as the *Codex Regius*, rediscovered in the mid–1600s. During his long career as an Oxford professor, J.R.R. Tolkien frequently lectured on the subject of the *Codex Regius*, and even wrote his own translation of portions of the document in his narrative poem, *The Legend of Sigurd and Gudrún*.

There are many beliefs about the origin of the elves. In Hall's *Elves in Anglo-Saxon England: Matters of Belief, Health, Gender and Identity*, they are identified with the lost children of Eve in an Icelandic folktale. (ibid; p. 75)

Leprechauns

Leprechauns are of the family of elves but are distinctly Irish. Leprechauns are shoemakers. This is why most elves and fairies put up with their trickster nature: after many nights of dancing, which is one of the fairies' favorite pastimes, they all need new shoes! Leprechauns provide these. Leprechauns live alone, preferring solitude, even from their own kind. They aren't comfortable with the lighthearted gaiety and fun that fairies indulge in. However, leprechauns are merry and have been heard to sing a song or two while making shoes.

Beyond shoemaking, Leprechauns have another specialty: they know where buried treasure lies, that "pot of gold" that is so famously associated with them. They also carry two coins in a little purse, one is magical and one is not. The magical one is always replaced when used or given away, and the other is not. As tricksters, leprechauns always give the ordinary coin to humans who manage to capture them, and while the human is looking at the coin, they escape. It is said that they can vanish in the blink of an eye. One must always keep an *opened* eye on a Leprechaun if one wants his magic coin or his hidden treasure.

They are not pretty like most elves, some of which are supremely beautiful; leprechauns are ugly. They smell foul, use foul language, and drink excessively, mostly beer in jugs. And they smoke, using a clay pipe called a *dúidín* (pronounced *du-deen*). Leprechauns are small and chunky, yet they are nimble! They can move very fast, and love to hide behind trees. Unlike the little green–clothed depictions we use today, the classical leprechaun wears a many–pocketed leather apron, a gray coat, and a red cocked hat. He almost always has a shoe and a hammer in his hands, or a beer and a pipe.

Fairies do not enjoy their company, but that's not a problem, because leprechauns don't enjoy the company of fairies either. Despite this, there is a close relationship between fairies and leprechauns beyond the need for new shoes. Leprechauns are the "bankers" and protectors of fairy treasures and fortunes. You see, in the lore and law of this invisible realm, all treasure belongs to the fairies and the fairies can spend it however they wish. However, fairies, especially trooping fairies, don't have any sense of the value of a coin or jewel, and they have little to no memory for what's already been spent—once out of sight, it's out of mind. Here's where the leprechauns help the fairies avoid bankruptcy, and why leprechauns are so good at hiding treasure. However, wherever a leprechaun hides a treasure of gold, a rainbow hovers over it! Giving a hint as to where a leprechaun's treasure may be. This causes leprechauns to suffer much from anxiety. If a being captures a leprechaun and never lets his eye off of him and demands the little guy's treasure, he must give it to him, and leprechauns always do. But few beings can keep their eye on him, because he is so tricky and clever, and a good storyteller as well as. Often a well-told story distracts his captor and the leprechaun is gone before you know it. However, there have been times when a leprechaun becomes so moved by an act of kindness or tenderness, that he offers the person a drink and a portion of his treasure, or even the magic coin in his purse. Remember, even though the coin has left the leprechaun's purse, it is always replaced with another one—that's the magic. And anyone carrying one of these magic coins is never without money.

Curiously, there are no female leprechauns. This adds to the mystery of leprechauns and where they come from or how many there are.

Nature Spirits

Nature Spirits are associated with the classic four elements of the physical world: earth, water, fire, and air.

- Gnomes are the spirits of earth;
- Undines (also called Ondines) are the spirits of water;
- Salamanders are the spirits of fire,;
- Sylphs are the spirits of the air (also called Sylphids—depicted as a type of fairy in the ballet *La Sylphide* and Shakespeare's *A Midsummer Night's Dream*).

Much of this information was gathered and published by Paracelsus in his alchemical writings of the early 1500s in Europe, and M.M. Pattison Muir published more in 1902 in his book, *The Story of Alchemy and the Beginnings of Chemistry*. In addition to the four elements the nature spirits are also *personified* in three other major life forms:

- Dryads are the spirits of vegetation;
- Fauns are the spirits of animal life;

- Nymphs are the spirits of the music and dance.

Native American "Little People"

I found it surprising to learn that most every Native American tribe has legend and lore about "little people":

The Cherokee of the Appalachian Mountain region have the *Nûñë'hï* (immortal spirit people) and the *Yunwi Tsunsdi* (spirits who live in rock caves on the mountain side).

The Choctaw of Southeastern North America have the *Bohpoli* (little sprites or hobgoblins) and *Kowi Anukasha* (literally, "the ones who stay in the woods").

The Crow of the Yellowstone River Valley have the *Nirumbee* or *Awwakkulé*, a race of ferocious goblin–like beings between one and two feet tall, with sharp teeth and squat necks. Nirumbee are generally enemies of humankind.

The Lakota nation has the *Canotila* (Canotina, Canoti), that are forest spirits usually appearing as sprites or dwarves. *Canoti* literally means "tree dweller," and *canotila* means "little tree dweller." They were considered messengers from the spirit world and often appeared to Lakota people in dreams.

Iroquois (which Cayce's discourse 1219-1 stated are the remnant of Atlantis!) have the *Gahongas*, one of the three types of spirits called the "Stone Throwers," and inhabit the rocky terrain and the rivers of the region. The other two spirits are the *Ohdows*, who are responsible for preventing the monsters of the underworld from escaping into the upper world of the people, and the *Gandayah*, who are responsible for the fertility of the earth and are the guardians of freshwater fish.

The Seminoles of Florida have the *Fastachee* or "Little Givers," who are corn spirits, usually appearing as dwarfs presenting the gift of corn.

The Wampanoag people have the *Pukwudgie*, a two–to–three–foot tall trouble–maker to be avoided. They were once friendly to humans, but then turned against them.

The Mohegans tell that the rocks of Mohegan Hill are the home of the *Makiawisug*, or little people. After nightfall, the call of the Whippoor–will signals their arrival. They are good spirits, but the Mohegans know they must be treated with respect, according to tradition. It is important to leave baskets of food, such as corn cakes and berries, or even meat in the woods for them. Wearing flowers for moccasins, they gather the gifts at night—in fact, Makiawisug means "Whip-poor-will moccasins." [Cited from http://www.mohegan.nsn.us/.]

5

❧◉❧

Reverend Kirk's "The Secret Commonwealth"

What you are about to read are excerpts from one of the classic sources for information on the little people. It was written in the late 1600s, in an English dialect that we will find somewhat difficult to read. The spelling, capitalization, and sentence structure were different than ours today, and in some cases the words are nearly impossible to discern. I've supplemented modern words where it seemed necessary and explained terms or references used—all of mine are in [brackets], while all comments in (parentheses) are the original author's. It was written by Reverend Robert Kirk, a Scottish Episcopalian minister in Aberfoyle, Scotland (spelled *Aberfoill* by Reverend Kirk), and completed in 1691. There is a letter by Lord Reay's to Mr. Samuel Pepys dated October 24, 1699, that affirms the existence of such a manuscript, stating: "I have got a manuscript since I last came to Scotland, whose author, though a parson, after giving a very full account of the Second

Sight (term used for "seeing fairies"), defends there being no sin in it." The only extant edition of Reverend Kirk's "The Secret Commonwealth" is dated 1815.

Why have I included excerpts from the manuscript in this book? The answer is that I wanted you to experience what I experienced when I first read the manuscript. It gives us such a direct connection to the human people in the 1600s and how they believed in and experienced the little people. And rather than transliterate the Reverend's Scottish English into our modern language, I felt a more intimate connection to him and his reporting by using his spellings, terms, and arrangement of thoughts in written sentences. Yes, it is difficult, even somewhat fatiguing, to read seventeenth century English, but taking my time I found that I could almost feel the man and his community, and their lives with the fairies.

My source is: Robert Kirk, *The Secret Commonwealth of Elves, Fauns, and Fairies*, Stirling: Eneas Mackay, 1933 (available through www.Sacred-Texts.com). This edition is a reprint of the 1893 edition, which in turn is based on the first printed edition in 1815. And as stated, Kirk's original manuscript dates to 1691, and was confirmed to exist by a letter dated 1699.

Reverend Robert Kirk earned his Masters of Arts at Edinburgh and his Doctorate in Theology at St. Andrews. Perhaps more directly related to his theme of fairies, fauns, elves, and other little people may be that he was a "seventh son." The folklore surrounding a seventh son in those times led people to believe him to have special powers. Of course, the greater powers were those of the seventh son of a seventh son, which Reverend Kirk was not. However, some believed that he was possibly a fairy who incarnated as a human to help us better understand them. And some believed that beneath his tombstone is an empty grave, because the fairies took him to fairyland upon his supposed human "death." None other than Sir Walter Scott, in his 1830s manuscript, *Demonology and Witchcraft*, referred to Reverend Kirk's manuscript, clearly adding to the importance of the work.

Reverend Kirk wrote on his title page:

The Secret Commonwealth
or,
A Treastise displayeing the Chiefe Curiosities
as they are in Use among diverse of the
People of Scotland to this Day;
SINGULARITIES for the most Part peculiar to
that Nation.

His opening paragraphs were:

These *Siths*, or Fairies, they call *Sleagh Maith*, or the Good People, it would seem, to prevent the Dint of their ill Attempts, (for the Irish use to bless all they fear Harme of) and are said to be of midle Nature betuixt Man and Angel [a belief common to many peoples beyond the Scottish], as were Daemons thought to be of old; of intelligent fluidious Spirits, and light changable Bodies (lyke those called Astral), somewhat of the nature of a condensed Cloud, and best seen in Twilight. Thes Bodies be so plyable thorough the Subtilty of the Spirits that agitate them, that they can make them appear or disappear att Pleasure. Some have Bodies or Vehicles so spungious [sponge-like, thus *absorbing* nourishment], thin, and delecat, that are fed by only sucking into some fine spirituous Liquors, that peirce lyke pure Air and Oyl [oil]: others feid [feed] more gross on the Foyson [*foison*, meaning "the physical energy and strength"] or substance of Corns and Liquors, or Corne it selfe that grows on the Surface of the Earth, which these Fairies steal away, partly invisible, partly preying on the Grain, as do Crowes and Mice; wherefore in this same Age, they are some times heard to bake Bread, strike Hammers, and do such lyke Services within the little Hillocks they most haunt: some whereof of old, before the Gospell dispelled Paganism [here we find the belief that Christianity was pushing the old pagan ways and wisdoms aside], and in some barbarous Places as yet, enter Houses after all are at rest, and set the Kitchens in order, cleansing all the Vessels. Such Drags [takers] goe under the name of Brownies.

When we have plenty, they have Scarcity at their Homes; and on the contrarie (for they are empowred to catch as much Prey everywhere as they please), there Robberies notwithstanding oft tymes occasion great Rickes of Corne not to bleed so weill, (as they call it), or prove to copious by verie farr as wes [was] expected by the Owner. [In those times it was believed that the fairies do not bodily take things, animals, or persons but only the strength and energy of it, causing the owners to get less life out of a thing, animal, or person than they expected. In Gaelic the term is *toradh*, which is something's or someone's essence, virtue, fruit, or benefit. The outward appearance is there, but the life essence is gone.]

There Bodies of congealled Air are some tymes caried aloft, other whiles grovell in different Schapes [shapes], and enter into any Cranie or Clift of the Earth where Air enters, to their ordinary Dwellings; the Earth being full of Cavities and Cells, and there being no Place nor Creature but is supposed to have other Animals (greater or lesser) living in or upon it as Inhabitants; and no such thing as a pure Wilderness in the whole Universe.

We then (the more terrestriall kind have now so numerously planted all Countreys), do labour for that abstruse People, as weill as for ourselves. Albeit, when severall Countreys were unhabitated by ws [us], these had their easy Tillage above Ground, as we now. [Kirk titled this section of his manuscript "Subterranean Inhabitants" and indicated that they once lived on the land, but after humans took over the land, they went into cracks, crevices, furrows, and other underground places.] The Print of those Furrous [furrows] do yet remaine to be seen on the Shoulders of very high Hills, which was done when the champayn Ground was Wood and Forrest.

They remove to other Lodgings at the Beginning of each Quarter of the Year, so traversing till Doomsday, being imputent [and impotent of?] staying in one Place, and finding some Ease by so purning [Journeying] and changing Habitations. Their chamaelion-lyke Bodies swim in the Air near the Earth with Bag and Bagadge; and at such revolution of Time, Seers, or Men of the SECOND SIGHT (Faemales being seldome so qualified) have very terrifying Encounters with them, even on High Ways; who therefoir uswally [usually] shune to travel abroad at these four Seasons of the Year, and thereby have made it a Custome to this Day among the Scottish-Irish to keep Church duely evry first Sunday of the Quarter to fene or hallow themselves, their Corns and Cattell, from the Shots and Stealth of these wandring Tribes; and many of these superstitious People will not be seen in Church againe till the nixt Quarter begin, as if no Duty were to be learned or done by them, but all the Use of Worship and Sermons were to save them from these Arrows that fly in the Dark.

Reverend Kirk's "Arrows that fly in the Dark" are the ancient flint arrowheads, which the witch Isabel Gowdie [in Pitcairn's *Scottish Criminal Trials*, 1720] confessed: "As for Elf arrows, the Divell sharpes them with his ain hand, and deliveris them to the Elf boys, wha whyttlis and dightis them with a sharp thing lyk a paking needle; bot when I was in Elfland, I saw them whittling and dighting them."

Reverend Kirk's comments about women being "seldom so qualified" and men having "very terrifying encounters" with fairies on the roads is because human women rarely traveled, and whenever they did it was in the company of menfolk protecting them. However, later in his manuscript, he gives examples of women who encountered fairies. Here are two:

Among other Instances of undoubted Verity, proving in these the Being of such aerial People, of Species of Creatures not vulgarly known, I add the subsequent Relations, some whereof I have from my Acquaintances with the Actors and Patients and the Rest from the Eye-witnesses to the Matter of Fact. The first whereof shall be of the Woman taken out of her Child-bed, and having a lingering Image of her substituted Bodie in her Roome [a commonly believed activity of fairies: taking human babies and replacing them with almost lifeless replicas who often die earlier than they should have], which Resemblance decay'd, dy'd, and was bur'd. But the Person stollen returning to her Husband after two Years Space [the replica had grown and married, then the real woman returned from fairyland], he being convinced by many undenyable Tokens that she was his former Wyfe, admitted her Home, and had diverse Children by her. Among other Reports she gave her Husband, this one: That she perceived little what they [fairies] did in the spacious House she lodg'd in, untill she anointed one of her Eyes with a certain Unction that was by her; which they perceiving to have acquainted her with their Actions, they fain'd her blind of that Eye with a Puff of their Breath. She found the Place full of Light, without any Fountain or Lamp from whence it did spring. This Person lived in the Countrey nixt to that of my last Residence, and might furnish Matter of Dispute amongst Casuists, whither if her Husband had been mary'd in the Interim of her two Years Absence, he was oblidged to divorse from the second Spouse, at the Return of the first. There is ane Airt, appearingly without Supersition, for recovering of such as are stolen, but think it superfluous to insert it.

In this next story, Kirk reports about an aged woman who though she did not eat much or sleep much always had strength. He tells her story with the implication that her rather unusual disposition and healthy balance may have been gained by experiences she had in the hills at nighttime looking after her sheep, noting that she claimed to have met and conversed with strange "people" and was once transported to another place.

I saw a Woman of fourtie Years of Age [life expectancy in the 1660s in Scotland and England was about 35 years], and examined her (having another Clergie Man in my Companie) about a Report that past of her long fasting. It was told by them of the House, as well as her selfe, that she tooke verie little or no Food for severall Years past; that she tarried in the Fields over Night, saw and conversed with a People she knew not, having wandered in seeking of her Sheep, and sleep't upon a Hillock, and finding her self transported to another Place before Day. The Woman had a Child since that Time, and is still prettie melanchollyous and silent, hardly ever seen to laugh. Her natural Heat and radical Moisture seem to be equally balanced, lyke ane unextinguished Lamp, and going in a Circle, not unlike to the faint of Lyfe of Bees, and some Sort of Birds, that sleep all the Winter over, and revive in the Spring.

In this next brief segment, Reverend Kirk gives us some more details into the lives of fairies:

> They are distributed in Tribes and Orders, and have Children, Nurses, Mariages, Deaths, and Burialls, in appearance, even as we, (unless they so do for a Mock-show, or to prognosticate some such Things among us.).

The implication here is that on occasion fairies would put on shows mocking human activities or reveal an upcoming human event that they foresaw through some knowing method of their own by displaying the event before humans in a show.

Andrew Lang (1844–1912)—a Scottish poet and novelist best known as a collector of folk and fairy tales—wrote and spoke about Kirk's book, noting these details about fairies:

> Although in modern culture they are often depicted as young, sometimes winged, humans of small stature, they originally were depicted quite differently: tall, radiant, angelic beings or short, wizened trolls being two of the commonly mentioned forms. Diminutive fairies of one kind or another have been recorded for centuries, but occur alongside the human-sized beings; these have been depicted as ranging in size from very tiny up to the size of a human child. Even with these small fairies, however, their small size may be magically assumed rather than constant. Some fairies though normally quite small were able to dilate their figures to imitate humans. Wings, while common in Victorian and later artwork of fairies, are very rare in the folklore; even very small fairies flew with magic, sometimes flying on ragwort stems or the backs of birds. Nowadays, fairies are often depicted with ordinary insect wings or butterfly wings. Various animals have also been described as fairies. Sometimes this is the result of shape shifting on part of the fairy, as in the case of the *selkie* (seal people); others, like the *kelpie* [Scottish name given to a shape-shifting water spirit inhabiting the lochs and pools of Scotland. It has usually been described as appearing as a horse, but is able to adopt human form. Some accounts state that the kelpie retains its hooves when appearing as a human, leading to its association with the

Christian idea of Satan as alluded to by Robert Burns in his 1786 poem "Address to the Deil".] and various black dogs, appear to stay more constant in form. In those days it was thought unwise to speak of one's knowledge of the fairy folk, for revelation of their secrets would incur their displeasure and subsequent infliction of punishment . . . it was commonly held that those who had been in some way close to fairies would end up in the fairy realm at the termination of their earthly existence. Rev. William M. Taylor reported that at the time of Rev. Kirk's death people believed that he had been taken by the fairies because he had been prying too deeply into their secrets. It is said that his headstone stands over an empty tomb. ["The History of the Book and Author," Andrew Lang Collection, St. Andrews]

Now back to Reverend Kirk's writing. In this section he defends his research on the fairies and gives us a little insight into the legends and lore that motivated him:

As our Religion oblidges us not to make a peremptory and curious Search into these Obtrusenesses, so that Histories of all Ages give as many plain Examples of extraordinary Occurrances as make a modest Inquiry not contemptable. How much is written of Pigme's, Fairies, Nymphs, Syrens, Apparitions, which tho not the tenth Part true, yet could not spring of nothing! Even English Authors relate Barry Island, in Glamorganshire, that laying your Ear into a Clift of the Rocks, blowing of Bellows, stricking of Hammers, clashing of Armour, fyling of Iron, will be heard distinctly ever since Merlin inchaunted [enchanted] those subterranean Wights [living creature] to a solid manuall forging of Arm's to Aurelius Ambrosius [a war leader who won an important battle against the Anglo-Saxons in the 5th century] and his Brittans, till he returned [legend holds that he returned in the 9th century]; which Merlin being killed in a Battell, and not coming to loose the Knot, these active Vulcans [when magic does not come to loose the knot of bondage, then fire gods and metalworkers at the forge must break the bonds] are there ty'd to a perpetuall Labour. But to dip no deeper than this . . .

As you can see, though these parsons were Christian ministers, they were well aware of ancient lore and mystical, magical events that affected the lives of their human community—even though such had its origin in so-called "paganism."

6

⚜

Excerpts from J.R.R. Tolkien's "On Fairy Stories"

ohn Ronald Reuel Tolkien (1892–1973) was a close friend to the novelist C.S. Lewis (1898–1963). Tolkien was an English writer, poet, philologist [one who studies languages in written historical sources], and a university professor. Of course, he is best known as the author of the classic fantasy works, *The Hobbit*, *The Lord of the Rings*, and *The Silmarillion*.

This essay we are about to read was initially written for a presentation that Tolkien gave for the Andrew Lang lecture series at the University of St. Andrews in 1939. It first appeared in print in 1947, in a volume compiled by none other than C.S. Lewis, titled, *Essays Presented to Charles Williams*.

Here are excerpts from the document. I have used ellipses to indicate where sections have been removed for our purposes and focus here. Asides in (parentheses) are Tolkien's and those in [brackets] are mine.

And though much of it is related to the writing of fairy stories, Tolkien includes much that I found to be helpful to our topic in this book. As with Reverend Kirk's manuscript, I have left Tolkien's writing style, spelling, capitalization, and sentence structure as he gave it:

> I PROPOSE to speak about fairy-stories, though I am aware that this is a rash adventure. Faerie is a perilous land, and in it are pitfalls for the unwary and dungeons for the overbold. And overbold I may be accounted, for though I have been a lover of fairy-stories since I learned to read, and have at times thought about them, I have not studied them professionally. I have been hardly more than a wandering explorer (or trespasser) in the land, full of wonder but not of information.
>
> The realm of fairy-story is wide and deep and high and filled with many things: all manner of beasts and birds are found there; shoreless seas and stars uncounted; beauty that is an enchantment, and an ever-present peril; both joy and sorrow as sharp as swords. In that realm a man may, perhaps, count himself fortunate to have wandered, but its very richness and strangeness tie the tongue of a traveller who would report them. And while he is there it is dangerous for him to ask too many questions, lest the gates should be shut and the keys be lost. . . .
>
> Supernatural is a dangerous and difficult word in any of its senses, looser or stricter. But to fairies it can hardly be applied, unless super is taken merely as a superlative prefix. For it is man who is, in contrast to fairies, supernatural (and often of diminutive stature); whereas they are natural, far more natural than he. Such is their doom. The road to fairyland is not the road to Heaven; nor even to Hell, I believe, though some have held that it may lead thither indirectly by the Devil's tithe.

O see ye not yon narrow road
So thick beset wi' thorns and briers?
That is the path of Righteousness,
Though after it but few inquires.

And see ye not yon braid, braid road

> That lies across the lily leven?
> That is the path of Wickedness,
> Though some call it the Road to Heaven.
>
> And see ye not yon bonny road
> That winds about yon fernie brae [hillside]?
> That is the road to fair Elfland,
> Where thou and I this nightmare gave.

As for diminutive size: I do not deny that the notion is a leading one in modern use. I have often thought that it would be interesting to try to find out how that has come to be so; but my knowledge is not sufficient for a certain answer. Of old there were indeed some inhabitants of Faerie that were small (though hardly diminutive), but smallness was not characteristic of that people as a whole. The diminutive being, elf or fairy, is (I guess) in England largely a sophisticated product of literary fancy. It is perhaps not unnatural that in England, the land where the love of the delicate and fine has often reappeared in art, fancy should in this matter turn towards the dainty and diminutive, as in France it went to court and put on powder and diamonds. Yet I suspect that this flower-and-butterfly minuteness was also a product of "rationalization," which transformed the glamour of Elfland into mere finesse, and invisibility into a fragility that could hide in a cowslip or shrink behind a blade of grass. It seems to become fashionable soon after the great voyages had begun to make the world seem too narrow to hold both men and elves . . .

I said the sense "stories about fairies" was too narrow. It is too narrow, even if we reject the diminutive size, for fairy-stories are not in normal English usage stories about fairies or elves, but stories about Fairy, that is Faerie, the realm or state in which fairies have their being. Faerie contains many things besides elves and fays, and besides dwarfs, witches, trolls, giants, or dragons: it holds the seas, the sun, the moon, the sky; and the earth, and all things that are in it: tree and bird, water and stone, wine and bread, and ourselves, mortal men, when we are enchanted.

Stories that are actually concerned primarily with "fairies," that is with creatures that might also in modern English be called "elves," are relatively rare, and as a rule not very interesting. Most good "fairy-stories" are about the adventures of men in the Perilous Realm or upon its shadowy marches. Naturally so; for if elves are true, and really exist independently of our tales about them, then this also is certainly true: elves are not primarily concerned with us, nor we with them. Our fates are sundered, and our paths seldom meet. Even upon the borders of Faerie we encounter them only at some chance crossing of the ways . . .

Origins

It is plain enough that fairy-stories (in wider or in narrower sense) are very ancient indeed. Related things appear in very early records; and they are found universally, wherever there is language. We are therefore obviously confronted with a variant of the problem that the archaeologist encounters, or the comparative philologist: with the debate between independent evolution (or rather invention) of the similar; inheritance from a common ancestry; and diffusion at various times from one or more centres. Most debates depend on an attempt (by one or both sides) at over-simplification; and I do not suppose that this debate is an exception. The history of fairy-stories is probably more complex than the physical history of the human race, and as complex as the history of human language. All three things: independent invention, inheritance, and diffusion, have evidently played their part in producing the intricate web of Story. It is now beyond all skill but that of the elves to unravel it . . .

Philology [study of language in written historical sources] has been dethroned from the high place it once had in this court of inquiry. Max Muller's view of mythology as a "disease of language" can be abandoned without regret. Mythology is not a disease at all, though it may like all human things become diseased. You might as well say that thinking is a disease of the mind. It would be more near the truth to say that languages, especially modern European languages, are a disease of mythology. But Language cannot, all the same, be dismissed. The incarnate mind, the tongue, and the tale are in our world coeval. The human mind, endowed with the powers of generalization and abstraction, sees not only green-grass, discriminating it from other things (and finding it fair to look upon), but sees that it is green as well as being grass. But how powerful, how stimulating to the very faculty that produced it, was the invention of the adjective: no spell or incantation in Faerie is more potent. And that is not surprising: such incantations might indeed be said to be only another view of adjectives, a part of speech in a mythical grammar. The mind that thought of light, heavy, grey, yellow, still, swift, also conceived of magic that would make heavy things light and able to fly, turn grey lead into yellow gold, and the still rock into a swift water. If it could do the one, it could do the other; it inevitably did both. When we can take green from grass, blue from heaven, and red from blood, we have already an enchanter's power—upon one plane; and the desire to wield that power in the world external to our minds awakes. It does not follow that we shall use that power well upon any plane. We may put a deadly green upon a man's face and produce a horror; we may make the rare and terrible blue moon to shine; or we may cause woods to spring with silver leaves and rams to wear fleeces of gold, and put hot fire into the belly of the cold worm. But in such "fantasy," as it is called, new form is made; Faerie begins; Man becomes a sub-creator.

An essential power of Faerie is thus the power of making immediately effective by the will the visions of "fantasy." Not all are beautiful or even wholesome, not at any rate the fantasies of fallen Man. And he has stained the elves who have this power (in verity or fable) with his own stain. This aspect of "mythology" —sub-creation, rather than either representation or symbolic interpretation of the beauties and terrors of the world—is, I think, too little considered . . .

Fantasy

The human mind is capable of forming mental images of things not actually present. The faculty of conceiving the images is (or was) naturally called Imagination. But in recent times, in technical not normal language, Imagination has often been held to be something higher than the mere image-making, ascribed to the operations of Fancy (a reduced and depreciatory form of the older word Fantasy); an attempt is thus made to restrict, I should say misapply, Imagination to "the power of giving to ideal creations the inner consistency of reality."

Ridiculous though it may be for one so ill-instructed to have an opinion on this critical matter, I venture to think the verbal distinction philologically inappropriate, and the analysis inaccurate. The mental power of image-making is one thing, or aspect; and it should appropriately be called Imagination. The perception of the image, the grasp of its implications, and the control, which are necessary to a successful expression, may vary in vividness and strength: but this is a difference of degree in Imagination, not a difference in kind. The achievement of the expression, which gives (or seems to give) "the inner consistency of reality," is indeed another thing, or aspect, needing another name: Art, the operative link between Imagination and the final result, Sub-creation. For my present purpose I require a word which shall embrace both the Sub-creative Art in itself and a quality of strangeness and wonder in the Expression, derived from the Image: a quality essential to fairy-story. I propose, therefore, to arrogate to myself the powers of Humpty-Dumpty, and to use Fantasy for this purpose: in a sense, that is, which combines with its older and higher use as an equivalent of Imagination the derived notions of "unreality" (that is, of unlikeness to the Primary World), of freedom from the domination of observed "fact," in short of the fantastic. I am thus not only aware but glad of the etymological and semantic connexions of fantasy with fantastic: with images of things that are not only "not actually present," but which are indeed not to be found in our primary world at all, or are generally believed not to be found there. But while admitting that, I do not assent to the depreciative tone. That the images are of things not in the primary world (if that indeed is possible) is a virtue, not a vice. Fantasy (in this sense) is, I think, not a lower but a higher form of Art, indeed the most nearly pure form, and so (when achieved) the most potent.

Fantasy, of course, starts out with an advantage: arresting

strangeness. But that advantage has been turned against it, and has contributed to its disrepute. Many people dislike being "arrested." They dislike any meddling with the Primary World, or such small glimpses of it as are familiar to them. They, therefore, stupidly and even maliciously confound Fantasy with Dreaming, in which there is no Art; and with mental disorders, in which there is not even control: with delusion and hallucination.

But the error or malice, engendered by disquiet and consequent dislike, is not the only cause of this confusion. Fantasy has also an essential drawback: it is difficult to achieve. Fantasy may be, as I think, not less but more sub-creative; but at any rate it is found in practice that "the inner consistency of reality" is more difficult to produce, the more unlike are the images and the rearrangements of primary material to the actual arrangements of the Primary World. It is easier to produce this kind of "reality" with more "sober" material. Fantasy thus, too often, remains undeveloped; it is and has been used frivolously, or only half-seriously, or merely for decoration: it remains merely "fanciful." Anyone inheriting the fantastic device of human language can say the green sun. Many can then imagine or picture it. But that is not enough—though it may already be a more potent thing than many a "thumbnail sketch" or "transcript of life" that receives literary praise.

To make a Secondary World inside which the green sun will be credible, commanding Secondary Belief, will probably require labour and thought, and will certainly demand a special skill, a kind of elvish craft. Few attempt such difficult tasks. But when they are attempted and in any degree accomplished then we have a rare achievement of Art: indeed narrative art, story- making in its primary and most potent mode.

In human art Fantasy is a thing best left to words, to true literature. In painting, for instance, the visible presentation of the fantastic image is technically too easy; the hand tends to outrun the mind, even to overthrow it. Silliness or morbidity are frequent results. It is a misfortune that Drama, an art fundamentally distinct from Literature, should so commonly be considered together with it, or as a branch of it. Among these misfortunes we may reckon the depreciation of Fantasy. For in part at least this depreciation

is due to the natural desire of critics to cry up the forms of literature or "imagination" that they themselves, innately or by training,
prefer. And criticism in a country that has produced so great a
Drama, and possesses the works of William Shakespeare, tends
to be far too dramatic. But Drama is naturally hostile to Fantasy.
Fantasy, even of the simplest kind, hardly ever succeeds in Drama,
when that is presented as it should be, visibly and audibly acted.
Fantastic forms are not to be counterfeited. Men dressed up as
talking animals may achieve buffoonery or mimicry, but they do
not achieve Fantasy. This is, I think, well illustrated by the failure
of the bastard form, pantomime. The nearer it is to "dramatized
fairy-story" the worse it is. It is only tolerable when the plot and its
fantasy are reduced to a mere vestigiary framework for farce, and
no "belief" of any kind in any part of the performance is required
or expected of anybody. This is, of course, partly due to the fact
that the producers of drama have to, or try to, work with mechanism to represent either Fantasy or Magic. I once saw a so-called
"children's pantomime," the straight story of Puss-in-Boots, with
even the metamorphosis of the ogre into a mouse. Had this been
mechanically successful it would either have terrified the specta-
tors or else have been just a turn of high-class conjuring. As it was,
though done with some ingenuity of lighting, disbelief had not so
much to be suspended as hanged, drawn, and quartered.

In Macbeth, when it is read, I find the witches tolerable: they
have a narrative function and some hint of dark significance;
though they are vulgarized, poor things of their kind. They are
almost intolerable in the play. They would be quite intolerable, if
I were not fortified by some memory of them as they are in the
story as read. I am told that I should feel differently if I had the
mind of the period, with its witch-hunts and witch-trials. But that
is to say: if I regarded the witches as possible, indeed likely, in the
Primary World; in other words, if they ceased to be "Fantasy." That
argument concedes the point. To be dissolved, or to be degraded,
is the likely fate of Fantasy when a dramatist tries to use it, even
such a dramatist as Shakespeare. Macbeth is indeed a work by a
playwright who ought, at least on this occasion, to have written a
story, if he had the skill or patience for that art.

A reason, more important, I think, than the inadequacy of stage-effects, is this: Drama has, of its very nature, already attempted a kind of bogus, or shall I say at least substitute, magic: the visible and audible presentation of imaginary men in a story. That is in itself an attempt to counterfeit the magician's wand. To introduce, even with mechanical success, into this quasimagical secondary world a further fantasy or magic is to demand, as it were, an inner or tertiary world. It is a world too much. To make such a thing may not be impossible. I have never seen it done with success. But at least it cannot be claimed as the proper mode of Drama, in which walking and talking people have been found to be the natural instruments of Art and illusion.

For this precise reason—that the characters, and even the scenes, are in Drama not imagined but actually beheld—Drama is, even though it uses a similar material (words, verse, plot), an art fundamentally different from narrative art. Thus, if you prefer Drama to Literature (as many literary critics plainly do), or form your critical theories primarily from dramatic critics, or even from Drama, you are apt to misunderstand pure story-making, and to constrain it to the limitations of stage-plays. You are, for instance, likely to prefer characters, even the basest and dullest, to things. Very little about trees as trees can be got into a play.

Now "Faerian Drama"—those plays which according to abundant records the elves have often presented to men—can produce Fantasy with a realism and immediacy beyond the compass of any human mechanism. As a result their usual effect (upon a man) is to go beyond Secondary Belief. If you are present at a Faerian drama you yourself are, or think that you are, bodily inside its Secondary World. The experience may be very similar to Dreaming and has (it would seem) sometimes (by men) been confounded with it. But in Faerian drama you are in a dream that some other mind is weaving, and the knowledge of that alarming fact may slip from your grasp. To experience directly a Secondary World: the potion is too strong, and you give to it Primary Belief, however marvellous the events. You are deluded— whether that is the intention of the elves (always or at any time) is another question. They at any rate are not themselves deluded. This is for them a form of Art, and distinct from Wizardry or Magic, properly so called. They do not live in it, though they can, perhaps, afford to spend more time at it than human artists can. The Primary World, Reality, of elves and men is the same, if differently valued and perceived.

We need a word for this elvish craft, but all the words that have been applied to it have been blurred and confused with other things. Magic is ready to hand, and I have used it above, but I should not have done so: Magic should be reserved for the operations of the Magician. Art is the human process that produces by the way (it is not its only or ultimate object) Secondary Belief. Art of the same sort, if more skilled and effortless, the elves can also use, or so the reports seem to show; but the more potent and specially elvish craft I will, for lack of a less debatable word, call Enchantment. Enchantment produces a Secondary World into which both designer and spectator can enter, to the satisfaction of their senses while they are inside; but in its purity it is artistic in desire and purpose. Magic produces, or pretends to produce, an alteration in the Primary World. It does not matter by whom it is said to be practised, fay or mortal, it remains distinct from the other two; it is not an art but a technique; its desire is power in this world, domination of things and wills.

To the elvish craft, Enchantment, Fantasy aspires, and when it is successful of all forms of human art most nearly approaches. At the heart of many man-made stories of the elves lies, open or concealed, pure or alloyed, the desire for a living, realized sub-creative art, which (however much it may outwardly resemble it) is inwardly wholly different from the greed for self-centred power which is the mark of the mere Magician. Of this desire the elves, in their better (but still perilous) part, are largely made; and it is from them that we may learn what is the central desire and aspiration of human Fantasy—even if the elves are, all the more in so far as they are, only a product of Fantasy itself. That creative desire is only cheated by counterfeits, whether the innocent but clumsy devices of the human dramatist, or the malevolent frauds of the magicians. In this world it is for men unsatisfiable, and so imperishable. Uncorrupted, it does not seek delusion nor be-witchment and domination; it seeks shared enrichment, partners in making and delight, not slaves.

To many, Fantasy, this sub-creative art which plays strange tricks with the world and all that is in it, combining nouns and redistributing adjectives, has seemed suspect, if not illegitimate. To some it has seemed at least a childish folly, a thing only for peoples or for persons in their youth. As for its legitimacy I will say no more than to quote a brief passage from a letter I once wrote to a man who described myth and fairy-story as "lies"; though to do him justice he was kind enough and confused enough to call fairy-story-making "Breathing a lie through Silver."

> "Dear Sir," I said—Although now long estranged,
> Man is not wholly lost nor wholly changed.
> Disgraced he may be, yet is not de-throned,
> and keeps the rags of lordship once he owned:
> Man, Sub-creator, the refracted Light
> through whom is splintered from a single White
> to many hues, and endlessly combined
> in living shapes that move from mind to mind.
> Though all the crannies of the world we filled
> with Elves and Goblins, though we dared to build
> Gods and their houses out of dark and light,
> and sowed the seed of dragons—'twas our right
> (used or misused). That right has not decayed:
> we make still by the law in which we're made."

Fantasy is a natural human activity. It certainly does not destroy or even insult Reason; and it does not either blunt the appetite for, nor obscure the perception of, scientific verity. On the contrary. The keener and the clearer is the reason, the better fantasy will it make. If men were ever in a state in which they did not want to know or could not perceive truth (facts or evidence), then Fantasy would languish until they were cured. If they ever get into that state (it would not seem at all impossible), Fantasy will perish, and become Morbid Delusion.

For creative Fantasy is founded upon the hard recognition that things are so in the world as it appears under the sun; on a recognition of fact, but not a slavery to it. So upon logic was founded the nonsense that displays itself in the tales and rhymes of Lewis Carroll. If men really could not distinguish between frogs and men, fairy-stories about frog-kings would not have arisen.

Fantasy can, of course, be carried to excess. It can be ill done. It can be put to evil uses. It may even delude the minds out of which it came. But of what human thing in this fallen world is that not true? Men have conceived not only of elves, but they have imagined gods, and worshipped them, even worshipped those most deformed by their authors' own evil. But they have made false gods out of other materials: their notions, their banners, their monies; even their sciences and their social and economic theories have demanded human sacrifice. *Abusus non tollit usum* ["does not preclude the use of"]. Fantasy remains a human right: we make in our measure and in our derivative mode, because we are made: and not only made, but made in the image and likeness of a Maker.

Recovery, Escape, Consolation

Recovery (which includes return and renewal of health) is a re-gaining—regaining of a clear view. I do not say "seeing things as they are" and involve myself with the philosophers, though I might venture to say "seeing things as we are (or were) meant to see them"—as things apart from ourselves. We need, in any case, to clean our windows; so that the things seen clearly may be freed from the drab blur of triteness or familiarity—from possessiveness. Of all faces those of our familiares are the ones both most difficult to play fantastic tricks with, and most difficult really to see with fresh attention, perceiving their likeness and unlikeness: that they are faces, and yet unique faces. This triteness is really the penalty of "appropriation": the things that are trite, or (in a bad sense) familiar, are the things that we have appropriated, legally or mentally. We say we know them. They have become like the things which once attracted us by their glitter, or their colour, or their shape, and we laid hands on them, and then locked them in our hoard, acquired them, and acquiring ceased to look at them.

Of course, fairy-stories are not the only means of recovery, or prophylactic against loss. Humility is enough. And there is (especially for the humble) Mooreeffoc [referring to things suddenly seen in a new or different angle], or Chestertonian ["paradoxical"] Fantasy. Mooreeffoc is a fantastic word, but it could be seen written up in every town in this land. It is Coffee-room, viewed from the inside through a glass door, as it was seen by Dickens on a dark London day; and it was used by Chesterton to denote the queerness of things that have become trite, when they are seen suddenly from a new angle. That kind of "fantasy" most people would allow to be wholesome enough; and it can never lack for material. But it has, I think, only a limited power; for the reason that recovery of freshness of vision is its only virtue. The word Mooreeffoc may cause you suddenly to realize that England is an utterly alien land, lost either in some remote past age glimpsed by history, or in some strange dim future to be reached only by a time-machine; to see the amazing oddity and interest of its inhabitants and their customs and feeding-habits; but it cannot do more than that: act as a time-telescope focused on one spot. Creative fantasy, because it is mainly trying to do something else (make something new), may open your hoard and let all the locked things fly away like cage-birds. The gems all turn into flowers or flames, and you will be warned that all you had (or knew) was dangerous and potent, not really effectively chained, free and wild; no more yours than they were you.

The "fantastic" elements in verse and prose of other kinds, even when only decorative or occasional, help in this release. But not so thoroughly as a fairy-story, a thing built on or about Fantasy, of which Fantasy is the core. Fantasy is made out of the Primary World, but a good craftsman loves his material, and has a knowledge and feeling for clay, stone and wood which only the art of making can give. By the forging of Gram cold iron was revealed; by the making of Pegasus horses were ennobled; in the Trees of the Sun and Moon root and stock, flower and fruit are manifested in glory.

And actually fairy-stories deal largely, or (the better ones) mainly, with simple or fundamental things, untouched by Fantasy, but these simplicities are made all the more luminous by their setting. For the story-maker who allows himself to be "free with" Nature can be her lover not her slave. It was in fairy-stories that I first divined the potency of the words, and the wonder of the things, such as stone, and wood, and iron; tree and grass; house and fire; bread and wine.

I will now conclude by considering Escape and Consolation, which are naturally closely connected. Though fairy-stories are of course by no means the only medium of Escape, they are today one of the most obvious and (to some) outrageous forms of "escapist" literature; and it is thus reasonable to attach to a consideration of them some considerations of this term "escape" in criticism generally.

I have claimed that Escape is one of the main functions of fairy-stories, and since I do not disapprove of them, it is plain that I do not accept the tone of scorn or pity with which "Escape" is now so often used: a tone for which the uses of the word outside literary criticism give no warrant at all. In what the misusers are fond of calling Real Life, Escape is evidently as a rule very practical, and may even be heroic. In real life it is difficult to blame it, unless it fails; in criticism it would seem to be the worse the better it succeeds. Evidently we are faced by a misuse of words, and also by a confusion of thought. Why should a man be scorned if, finding himself in prison, he tries to get out and go home? Or if, when he cannot do so, he thinks and talks about other topics than jailers and prison-walls? The world outside has not become less real because the prisoner cannot see it. In using escape in this way the critics have chosen the wrong word, and, what is more, they are confusing, not always by sincere error, the Escape of the Prisoner with the Flight of the Deserter. Just so a Party-spokesman might have labelled departure from the misery of the Fuhrer's or any other Reich and even criticism of it as treachery. In the same way these critics, to make confusion worse, and so to bring into contempt their opponents, stick their label of scorn not only on to Desertion, but on to real Escape, and what are often its companions, Disgust, Anger, Condemnation, and Revolt. Not only do they confound the escape of the prisoner with the flight of the deserter;

but they would seem to prefer the acquiescence of the "quisling" to the resistance of the patriot. To such thinking you have only to say "the land you loved is doomed" to excuse any treachery, indeed to glorify it.

For a trifling instance: not to mention (indeed not to parade) electric street-lamps of massproduced pattern in your tale is Escape (in that sense). But it may, almost certainly does, proceed from a considered disgust for so typical a product of the Robot Age, that combines elaboration and ingenuity of means with ugliness, and (often) with inferiority of result. These lamps may be excluded from the tale simply because they are bad lamps; and it is possible that one of the lessons to be learnt from the story is the realization of this fact. But out comes the big stick: "Electric lamps have come to stay," they say. Long ago Chesterton truly remarked that, as soon as he heard that anything "had come to stay," he knew that it would be very soon replaced—indeed regarded as pitiably obsolete and shabby. "The march of Science, its tempo quickened by the needs of war, goes inexorably on . . . making some things obsolete, and foreshadowing new developments in the utilization of electricity": an advertisement. This says the same thing only more menacingly. The electric street-lamp may indeed be ignored, simply because it is so insignificant and transient. Fairy-stories, at any rate, have many more permanent and fundamental things to talk about. Lightning, for example. The escapist is not so subservient to the whims of evanescent fashion as these opponents. He does not make things (which it may be quite rational to regard as bad) his masters or his gods by worshipping them as inevitable, even "inexorable." And his opponents, so easily contemptuous, have no guarantee that he will stop there: he might rouse men to pull down the street-lamps. Escapism has another and even wickeder face: Reaction.

Not long ago—incredible though it may seem—I heard a clerk of Oxenford declare that he "welcomed" the proximity of mass-production robot factories, and the roar of self-obstructive mechanical traffic, because it brought his university into "contact with real life." He may have meant that the way men were living and working in the twentieth century was increasing in barbarity at an alarming rate, and that the loud demonstration of this in the streets of Oxford might serve as a warning that it is not possible to preserve for long an oasis of sanity in a desert of unreason by mere fences, without actual offensive action (practical and intellectual). I fear he did not. In any case the expression "real life" in this context seems to fall short of academic standards. The notion that motor-cars are more "alive" than, say, centaurs or dragons is curious; that they are more "real" than, say, horses is pathetically absurd. How real, how startlingly alive is a factory chimney compared with an elm-tree: poor obsolete thing, insubstantial dream of an escapist!

"The rawness and ugliness of modern European life"—that real life whose contact we should welcome —"is the sign of a biological inferiority, of an insufficient or false reaction to environment." The maddest castle that ever came out of a giant's bag in a wild Gaelic story is not only much less ugly than a robot-factory, it is also (to use a very modern phrase) "in a very real sense" a great deal more real. Why should we not escape from or condemn the "grim Assyrian" absurdity of top-hats, or the Morlockian horror of factories? They are condemned even by the writers of that most escapist form of all literature, stories of Science fiction. These prophets often foretell (and many seem to yearn for) a world like one big glass-roofed railway-station. But from them it is as a rule very hard to gather what men in such a world-town will do. They may abandon the "full Victorian panoply" for loose garments (with zip-fasteners), but will use this freedom mainly, it would appear, in order to play with mechanical toys in the soon-cloying game of moving at high speed. To judge by some of these tales they will still be as lustful, vengeful, and greedy as ever; and the ideals of their idealists hardly reach farther than the splendid notion of building more towns of the same sort on other planets. It is indeed an age of "improved means to deteriorated ends." It is part of the essential malady of such days— producing the desire to escape, not indeed from life, but from our present time and self-made misery— that we are acutely conscious both of the ugliness of our works, and of their evil. So that to us evil and ugliness seem indissolubly allied. We find it difficult to conceive of evil and beauty together. The fear of the beautiful fay that ran through the elder ages almost eludes our grasp. Even more alarming: goodness is itself bereft of its proper beauty. In Faerie one can indeed conceive of an ogre who possesses a castle hideous as a nightmare (for the evil of the ogre wills it so), but one cannot conceive of a house built with a good purpose—an inn, a hostel for travellers, the hall of a virtuous and noble king—that is yet sickeningly ugly. At the present day it would be rash to hope to see one that was not—unless it was built before our time.

This, however, is the modern and special (or accidental) "escapist" aspect of fairy-stories, which they share with romances, and other stories out of or about the past. Many stories out of the past have only become "escapist" in their appeal through surviving from a time when men were as a rule delighted with the work of their hands into our time, when many men feel disgust with man- made things.

But there are also other and more profound "escapisms" that have always appeared in fairytale and legend. There are other things more grim and terrible to fly from than the noise, stench, ruthlessness, and extravagance of the internal-combustion engine. There are hunger, thirst, poverty, pain, sorrow, injustice, death. And even when men are not facing hard things such as these, there are ancient limitations from which fairy-stories offer a sort of escape, and old ambitions and desires (touching the very roots of fantasy) to which they offer a kind of satisfaction and consolation. Some are pardonable weaknesses or curiosities: such as the desire to visit, free as a fish, the deep sea; or the longing for the noiseless, gracious, economical flight of a bird, that longing which the aeroplane cheats, except in rare moments, seen high and by wind and distance noiseless, turning in the sun: that is, precisely when imagined and not used. There are profounder wishes: such as the desire to converse with other living things. On this desire, as ancient as the Fall, is largely founded the talking of beasts and creatures in fairy-tales, and especially the magical understanding of their proper speech. This is the root, and not the "confusion" attributed to the minds of men of the unrecorded past, an alleged "absence of the sense of separation of ourselves from beasts."

A vivid sense of that separation is very ancient; but also a sense that it was a severance: a strange fate and a guilt lies on us. Other creatures are like other realms with which Man has broken off relations, and sees now only from the outside at a distance, being at war with them, or on the terms of an uneasy armistice. There are a few men who are privileged to travel abroad a little; others must be content with travellers' tales. Even about frogs. In speaking of that rather odd but widespread fairy-story The Frog-King Max Muller asked in his prim way: "How came such a story ever to be invented? Human beings were, we may hope, at all times sufficiently enlightened to know that a marriage between a frog and the daughter of a queen was absurd." Indeed we may hope so! For if not, there would be no point in this story at all, depending as it does essentially on the sense of the absurdity. Folk-lore origins (or guesses about them) are here quite beside the point. It is of little avail to consider totemism. For certainly, whatever customs or beliefs about frogs and wells lie behind this story, the frogshape was and is preserved in the fairy-story precisely because it was so queer and the marriage absurd, indeed abominable. Though, of course, in the versions which concern us, Gaelic, German, English, there is in fact no wedding between a princess and a frog: the frog was an enchanted prince. And the point of the story lies not in thinking frogs possible mates, but in the necessity of keeping promises (even those with intolerable consequences) that, together with observing prohibitions, runs through all Fairyland. This is one of the notes of the horns of Elfland, and not a dim note.

And lastly there is the oldest and deepest desire, the Great Escape: the Escape from Death. Fairy- stories provide many examples and modes of this—which might be called the genuine escapist, or (I would say) fugitive spirit. But so do other stories (notably those of scientific inspiration), and so do other studies. Fairy-stories are made by men not by fairies. The Human-stories of the elves are doubtless full of the Escape from Deathlessness. But our stories cannot be expected always to rise above our common level. They often do. Few lessons are taught more clearly in them than the burden of that kind of immortality, or rather endless serial living, to which the "fugitive" would fly. For the fairy-story is specially apt to teach such things, of old and still today.

But the "consolation" of fairy-tales has another aspect than the imaginative satisfaction of ancient desires. Far more important is the Consolation of the Happy Ending. Almost I would venture to assert that all complete fairy-stories must have it. At least I would say that Tragedy is the true form of Drama, its highest function; but the opposite is true of Fairy-story. Since we do not appear to possess a word that expresses this opposite—I will call it Eucatastrophe. The eucatastrophic [from Greek meaning "good destruction," in the sense of a sudden happy turn in a story which pierces you with a joy that brings tears] tale is the true form of fairy-tale, and its highest function.

The consolation of fairy-stories, the joy of the happy ending: or more correctly of the good catastrophe, the sudden joyous "turn" (for there is no true end to any fairy-tale): this joy, which is one of the things which fairy-stories can produce supremely well, is not essentially "escapist," nor "fugitive." In its fairy-tale—or otherworld—setting, it is a sudden and miraculous grace: never to be counted on to recur. It does not deny the existence of dyscatastrophe [tragedy], of sorrow and failure: the possibility of these is necessary to the joy of deliverance; it denies (in the face of much evidence, if you will) universal final defeat and in so far is evangelium, giving a fleeting glimpse of Joy, Joy beyond the walls of the world, poignant as grief. It is the mark of a good fairy-story, of the higher or more complete kind, that however wild its events, however fantastic or terrible the adventures, it can give to child or man that hears it, when the "turn" comes, a catch of the breath, a beat and lifting of the heart, near to (or indeed accompanied by) tears, as keen as that given by any form of literary art, and having a peculiar quality. Even modern fairy-stories can produce this effect sometimes. It is not an easy thing to do; it depends on the whole story which is the setting of the turn, and yet it reflects a glory backwards. A tale that in any measure succeeds in this point has not wholly failed, whatever flaws it may possess, and whatever mixture or confusion of purpose. It happens even in Andrew Lang's own fairy-story, Prince Prigio, unsatisfactory in many ways as that is. When "each knight came alive and lifted his sword and shouted 'long live Prince Prigio,' " the joy has a little of that strange mythical fairy-story quality, greater than the event described. It would have none in Lang's tale, if the event described were not a piece of more serious fairy-story "fantasy" than the main bulk of the story, which is in general more frivolous, having the half-mocking smile of the courtly, sophisticated Conte. Far more powerful and poignant is the effect in a serious tale of Faerie. In such stories when the sudden "turn" comes we get a piercing glimpse of joy, and heart's desire, that for a moment passes outside the frame, rends indeed the very web of story, and lets a gleam come through.

> "Seven long years I served for thee,
> The glassy hill I clamb for thee,
> The bluidy shirt I wrang for thee,
> And wilt thou not wauken and turn to me?"
> He heard and turned to her.

This "joy" which I have selected as the mark of the true fairy-story (or romance), or as the seal upon it, merits more consideration.

Probably every writer making a secondary world, a fantasy, every sub-creator, wishes in some measure to be a real maker, or hopes that he is drawing on reality: hopes that the peculiar quality of this secondary world (if not all the details) are derived from Reality, or are flowing into it. If he indeed achieves a quality that can fairly be described by the dictionary definition: "inner consistency of reality," it is difficult to conceive how this can be, if the work does not in some way partake of reality. The peculiar quality of the "joy" in successful Fantasy can thus be explained as a sudden glimpse of the underlying reality or truth. It is not only a "consolation" for the sorrow of this world, but a satisfaction, and an answer to that question, "Is it true?" The answer to this question that I gave at first was (quite rightly): "If you have built your little world well, yes: it is true in that world." That is enough for the artist (or the artist part of the artist). But in the "eucatastrophe" we see in a brief vision that the answer may be greater—it may be a far- off gleam or echo of evangelium in the real world. The use of this word gives a hint of my epilogue. It is a serious and dangerous matter. It is presumptuous of me to touch upon such a theme; but if by grace what I say has in any respect any validity, it is, of course, only one facet of a truth incalculably rich: finite only because the capacity of Man for whom this was done is finite.

I would venture to say that approaching the Christian Story from this direction, it has long been my feeling (a joyous feeling) that God redeemed the corrupt making-creatures, men, in a way fitting to this aspect, as to others, of their strange nature. The Gospels contain a fairy-story, or a story of a larger kind which embraces all the essence of fairy-stories. They contain many marvels—peculiarly artistic, beautiful, and moving: "mythical" in their perfect, self-contained significance; and among the marvels is the greatest and most complete conceivable eucatastrophe. But this story has entered History and the primary world; the desire and aspiration of sub-creation has been raised to the fulfillment of Creation. The Birth of Christ is the eucatastrophe of Man's history. The Resurrection is the eucatastrophe of the story of the Incarnation. This story begins and ends in joy. It has pre-eminently the "inner consistency of reality." There is no tale ever told that men would rather find was true, and none which so many sceptical men have accepted as true on its own merits. For the Art of it has the supremely convincing tone of Primary Art, that is, of Creation. To reject it leads either to sadness or to wrath.

It is not difficult to imagine the peculiar excitement and joy that one would feel, if any specially beautiful fairy-story were found to be "primarily" true, its narrative to be history, without thereby necessarily losing the mythical or allegorical significance that it had possessed. It is not difficult, for one is not called upon to try and conceive anything of a quality unknown. The joy would have exactly the same quality, if not the same degree, as the joy which the "turn" in a fairy-story gives: such joy has the very taste of primary truth. (Otherwise its name would not be joy.) It looks forward (or backward: the direction in this regard is unimportant) to the Great Eucatastrophe. The Christian joy, the Gloria, is of the same kind; but it is preeminently (infinitely, if our capacity were not finite) high and joyous. But this story is supreme; and it is true. Art has been verified. God is the Lord, of angels, and of men—and of elves. Legend and History have met and fused.

But in God's kingdom the presence of the greatest does not depress the small. Redeemed Man is still man. Story, fantasy, still go on, and should go on. The Evangelium has not abrogated legends; it has hallowed them, especially the "happy ending." The Christian has still to work, with mind as well as body, to suffer, hope, and die; but he may now perceive that all his bents and faculties have a purpose, which can be redeemed. So great is the bounty with which he has been treated that he may now, perhaps, fairly dare to guess that in Fantasy he may actually assist in the effoliation [the removal or fall of the foliage] and multiple enrichment of creation. All tales may come true; and yet, at the last, redeemed, they may be as like and as unlike the forms that we give them as Man, finally redeemed, will be like and unlike the fallen that we know.

7

⚜

Encounters with Little People

As a child, Edgar Cayce often saw the usually invisible beings. On one occasion, his longtime stenographer, Gladys Davis, took down in shorthand Edgar Cayce's recollections of his childhood experience with his mother's sister Lou, who did not like it when Eddie (as he was called at around nine years of age) saw impossible scenes and little people! Here's that record as dictated to Gladys in 1938. Gladys typed it up in the form of a story:

"Come, Eddie. Don't you wish to help Auntie gather some greens for dinner? I think I saw some lovely wild mustard as I came through the field from Uncle Jim's the other evening."

As the boy and his aunt went through the lot by the barn, where many unusual things had happened to Eddie—or so he thought—he began to speak to his aunt about them.

"Auntie, I love to play in that barn, I have just lots of fun there!"

107

"Fun? Fun?" asked the aunt. "What is fun? You are not old enough to know what fun is, are you? What is so funny about the old barn?"

"Well," said the boy, "that is where Grandpa used to keep his tobacco, that he got so much money for. There is the old beam they used to prize the tobacco with. It is fun to go there and see the pole go up and down, and hear someone cry, 'Up! Down! Up! Down! Up! Down!' And there is a blue jay with a nest there; I saw her building it this morning. And there is one speckled egg in the nest already. I saw a wren also, looking at the horn Grandpa used to call the boys with, from the field."

"But," said the aunt, "They haven't prized tobacco there in a long time! And you never saw tobacco prized anyway, I'm sure."

"Yes I have!" said the boy. "I see Grandpa there every day when I go there to play, and besides there are a lot of little boys and girls that come there to play with me, and they can climb all over the barn and tell me what is on every pole in the barn!"

"Eddie, you shouldn't let your imagination run away with you like that! You are just imagining things! Don't you know it is wicked to tell stories?"

"What is being wicked, Auntie? I play with the children, that I know; and I see Grandpa, and he talks to me—as he has talked to the colored men who prize tobacco. What is wicked? I see it, and it is great fun for me! What is being wicked? Is that wicked, because I see them and say I see them?"

"If you saw them it would be alright," said the aunt, "but they are not there. Your grandfather has been dead for six years now, and dead people do not prize tobacco. So, to say that you do see them is wicked. I will have to speak to your mother about that."

"Oh, but Mother sees the children too!" said the boy. "She just hasn't been here when Grandpa was prizing tobacco."

"I don't believe it! And you are just a bad boy that likes to imagine things! I will speak to your mother. She must not humor you in all this tomfoolery!"

But they went on to the field and found plenty of nice wild mustard, and gathered a basket full.

Coming back toward the barn the aunt asked the boy again,

"Why do you say it is fun to play in the old barn?"

"Because," said the boy, "I have so many to play with there, and Grandpa is great fun. He tells me a lot of funny stories of what happened before the war, and during the war, and afterward."

"Are you sure it is your grandfather?"

"Of course it is Grandpa! I have felt his chin whiskers, and that is the way I used to tell him from Grandma when it was dark." "You are certainly a strange child," said the aunt. "I will have a talk with your mother. This thing must not go on else everyone will know you have gone beside yourself. It gives me the creeps to hear you talk like that!"

"Carrie," said the aunt that evening, as the boy was out at play, "what is this Eddie says about you seeing children playing with him in the barn? There are no children that live anywhere near here! You'd better take that child to the doctor! I think he is just out of his mind! He is not normal, some way!

"But Lou, I have seen the children Eddie speaks of. They can't harm him, I am sure."

"Whose children are they?"

"I do not know. They seem very nice, and I think Eddie is having an experience such as we read of but think can never come to us. I am praying about it, Lou, and I am sure no harm can come of it."

"But what about his saying that he sees and talks with his Grandpa. You know that is out of the question, and what will the neighbors say if they hear about all this foolishness? You need to give that boy a good thrashing, and stop all this fairy business or whatever you choose to call it!"

"Lou, I couldn't whip him for that! He is sure he sees all this, and I have seen the children myself. It is not just imagination. I do not know what it is, but I simply can't whip him for such as that. I just wish there was some way Eddie could go to church, study his Bible, and learn what this is all about."

"Tommyrot!" said Lou. "You don't mean to tell me you think this foolishness is of God! It is more like the Devil, if you don't mind my saying so, and certainly no good can come of such a thing! You had better take the child to the doctor. They will have nothing to do with him at any church, I can assure you!"

The aunt was married that summer and went to the eastern part
of the State to live, and didn't see Eddie for several years.
The next January Eddie's mother asked him if he would like to
go to Sunday school. So he began to go. The lesson was the first
of Genesis, the creation, and Eddie found it very interesting, in
fact, all absorbing. He asked his father to procure a book for him
that had the whole story in it. A few weeks later the Bible was
procured—the gift of a book dealer to whom the father told the
story.

Eddie began to read, and the more he read the more sure he became that these happenings in the barn were real and not foolish.
Yet, as others questioned him, the more of a recluse he became.

That year Eddie with his family moved to a little house in the
edge of a wood, one with a great variety of vegetation. There were
large oaks, hickory, white oak, poplar and beech in timber wood;
as well as hazelnuts, pawpaw, and many other fruit and nut trees.
Eddie became acquainted with all the beautiful dells and glades in
that wood, and built himself a retreat in a very pretty spot a quarter
of a mile from their house. There he kept his Bible, and read it
every day, reading and re-reading many portions of it.

After a few months of study, one afternoon he had an experience. He had been reading of the vision of Manoah, the father of
Samson. Eddie loved the story of Samson. Suddenly there was a
humming sound outside, and a bright light filled the little place
where Eddie sat. A figure appeared, all in white, bright as the
noonday light, and spoke, saying:

"Your prayers have been heard! What would you ask of me, that
I may give it to you?"

"Just that I may be helpful to others," answered Eddie, "especially to children who are ill; and that I may love my fellow man."
The figure disappeared.

In school next day Eddie missed his lessons as usual, and had
to remain to write the word "cabin" five hundred times on the
blackboard. When he got home, that evening his father was wait-
ing for him. Eddie studied his lessons that evening but seemed
unable to concentrate. Around eleven o'clock he had the first
experience of hearing the voice within, and it recalled the voice

of the visitor of the afternoon before. The voice said, "Sleep, and we may help you."

Eddie asked his father to let him sleep five minutes. He slept, and at the end of the time he knew every word in that particular spelling book, and as if he had a photographic image of the book he also knew on what page the words appeared!

From the time he was a very little boy, Edgar Cayce could see fairies, sprites, angels, and invisible friends. As a child, he thought that everyone was seeing them, but as he grew older, he learned that it wasn't so. He began to keep quiet about his abilities, because they caused unpleasant reactions in others, even his auntie, and ridicule of him and his family. When he became a more self-confident adult, he shared these recollections, one of which follows, and his stenographer Gladys recorded it thusly:

" . . . I remember so distinctly the garden at my mother's old home place when I was a very small child. My mother's father was one of the first settlers in southwestern Kentucky; had a fine old place, and the old-fashioned garden, with all the old-fashioned flowers, was known throughout that part of the country. Your mentioning your mother destroying bleeding hearts [flowers] calls to my mind what beautiful bunches of these grew in that garden, with a large bunch of striped grass, some very old peonies, all kinds of buttercups, and the like; a gorgeous bed of sweet violets, and all those old flowers. . . It was here that often in my early childhood, I met and played with those that others could never see. . .

These are at least some of my experiences. As to just what was the first experience, I don't know. The one that appears at present to be among the first, was when I was possibly eighteen or twenty months old. I had a playhouse in the back of an old garden, among the honeysuckle and other flowers. At that particular time much of this garden had grown up in tall reeds, as I remember. I had made a little shelter of the tops of the reeds, and had been assisted by an unseen playmate in weaving or fastening them together so they would form a shelter. On pretty days I played there. One afternoon my mother came down the garden walk calling me. My playmate (who appeared to me to be about the same size as myself) was with me. It had never occurred to me that he was not real, or that he wasn't one of the neighbors' children, until my mother spoke and asked me my playmate's name. I turned to ask him but he disappeared. For a time this disturbed my mother somewhat, and she questioned me at length. I remember crying because she had spied upon me several times, and each time the playmate would disappear.

About a year or eighteen months later, this was changed considerably—as to the number of playmates. We had moved to another country home. Here I had two favorite places where I played with these unseen people. One very peculiarly was in an old graveyard where the cedar trees had grown up. Under a cedar tree, whose limbs had grown very close to the ground, I made another little retreat, where—with these playmates—I gathered bits of colored glass, beautifully colored leaves and things of that nature from time to time. But, what disturbed me was that I didn't know where they [the playmates] came from or why they left when some of my family approached. The other retreat was a favorite old straw stack that I used to slide down. This was on the opposite side of the road (main highway) from where we lived, and in front of the house. The most outstanding experience (and one that I am sure disturbed her much) was when my mother looked out a window and saw children sliding down this straw stack with me. Of course, I had a lovely little retreat dug out under the side of the straw ring, in which we often sat and discussed the mighty problems of a three or four year old child. As my mother looked out, she called to ask who were the children playing with me. I realized I didn't know their names. How were they dressed, you ask? There were boys and girls. It would be impossible (at this date) to describe their dress, figure or face, yet it didn't then—nor does it now—occur to me that they were any different from myself, except that they had the ability to appear or disappear as our moods changed. Just once I looked out the window from the house and saw the fairies there, beckoning me to come and play. That time also my mother saw them very plainly, but she didn't make any objection to my going out to play with them. This experience, as I remember now, lasted during a whole season—or summer.

A few years afterwards (when I had grown to be six or seven years old) our home was in a little wood. Here I learned to talk with the trees, or it appeared that they talked with me. I even yet hold that anyone may hear voices, apparently coming from a tree, if willing to choose a tree (a living tree, not a dead one) and sit against it for fifteen to twenty minutes each day (the same time each day) for twenty days. This was my experience. I chose a very lovely tree, and around it I played with my playmates that came (who then seemed very much smaller than I). We built a beautiful bower of hazelnut branches, redwood, dogwood and the like, with wild violets, Jack-in-the-Pulpit, and many of the wild mosses that seemed to be especially drawn to this particular little place where I met my friends to talk with—the little elves of the trees. How often these came, I don't know. We lived there for several years. It was there that I read the Bible through the first time, that I learned to pray, that I had many visions or experiences; not only of vision-ing the elves but what seemed to me to be the hosts [angels] that must have appeared to the people of old, as recorded in Genesis particularly. In this little bower there was never any intrusion from those outside. It was here that I read the first letter from a girl-friend. It was here that I went to pray when my grandmother died, whom I loved so dearly and who had meant so much to me. To describe these elves of the trees, the fairies of the woods, or—to me—the angels or hosts, with all their beautiful and glorious sur-roundings, would be almost a sacrilege. They have meant, and do yet, so very much to me that they are as rather the sacred experi-ences that we do not speak of—any more than we would of our first kiss, and the like. Why do I draw such comparisons? There are, no doubt, physical manifestations that are a counterpart or an expression of all the unseen forces about us, yet we have closed our eyes and our ears to the songs of the spheres, so that we are unable again to hear the voices or to see the forms take shape and minister—yea strengthen us—day by day!

Possibly there are many questions you would ask as to what games we played. Those I played with at the haystack were differ-ent from those in the graveyard, or in the garden. Those I played with in the wood were different. They seemed to fit more often to what would interest or develop me. To say they planted the flowers or selected the bower, or the little cove in which my retreat was built, I don't think would be stretching it at all, or that they tended these or showed me—or talked to me of—their beauty. It was here that I first learned to read. Possibly the hosts on high gave me my first interpretation of that we call the Good Book. I do not think I am stretching my imagination when I say such a thing. We played the games of children, we played being sweethearts, we played being man and wife, we played being sisters and brothers, and we played being visitors and preachers. We played being policemen and the culprits. We played being all the things that we knew about us.

"I never have any of these visions now, or, if any, very rarely."

464-12, Report

When Cayce was fifty-four years old, he had a dream in which these same fairies and elves appeared to him again. His psychic reading on this dream explained that these were warnings that his soul would likely return to the spirit realms if his mind did not become more active in this world and find more people requesting his unique services. (294-128)

I find it most enlightening to hear people's encounters with the mystical beings, so here are some of the stories I've been told.

This next encounter was shared by a friend of mine.

My friend tells the story of being interested in Devas (sprites or little angelic beings) ever since reading about the possibility of such creatures in the Edgar Cayce material. According to this friend, once he found out about them, he always set aside a place in his yard or garden and told the Devas it was theirs to do with as they wished. After a number of years of talking to the plant Devas, he was at a neighbor's house and found himself sharing his interests in Devas. The neighbor told my friend that there was a small tree in the yard that had been planted within the last 2–3 years about four feet away from the water and always looked ill. The neighbor liked the tree's location but was worried it wouldn't survive. He asked my friend if it would be possible for him to go speak with the tree Devas and ask what was wrong with it?

My friend agreed, even though he didn't know if anything would happen. According to my friend: "I went and put my hands on the tree's trunk and closed my eyes. I got quiet for a moment, relaxed, and in my mind told the tree Devas that I wanted to help the tree and asked if they could somehow tell me what was wrong. Almost immediately I felt energy around me and even thought I could see (with my eyes closed) some sparkling lights. The next thing I saw in my mind was a repeating image of strong gusts of north wind blowing against the tree. The image repeated itself over and over again—a strong gust of north wind. The next thing I saw was a blockade or fence on the north side of the tree protecting it from the north wind for a few years until the tree was more mature."

When the experience was over, my friend told his neighbor about the vision he had. The neighbor agreed to build a v-shaped fence about five feet tall on the north side to help the tree. A few years later, the tree had matured and no longer appeared sickly.

Here's an interesting little tale of how a grandmother intentionally generated "fairy responses" only to ultimately experience them:

"I had never given fairies a thought growing up, not that I believed or didn't, I am pretty sure I only knew of one fairy, her name was Tinkerbell, and she probably lived in the castle at Disney World. Several years ago my granddaughters were coming over to stay for the weekend as they often did, and I always tried to have something fun or crafty lined up for them to enjoy. I had removed on old bird house from the yard that I thought they could enjoy repainting and crafting. It started out to be a toad house for the flower garden but before all was said and done they had turned the old bird house into a beautiful charming fairie cottage. They were so excited about hanging it outside and left a note to the fairies tucked inside the cottage door. They just knew that the fairies would be so pleased that they would come for a visit tonight while they slept. So, to make it real for them, I became their fairy grandmother and placed two acorns inside the back door of the cottage that night. The girls were beside themselves the next morning when they found them. We left Scrabble game letters out one night on a large stone below the fairy cottage and the girls left a note for the fairies, asking what their names were. The next morning the Scrabble letters spelled out Twinkles and Buttercup. It has become years now of leaving enchanted gifts from the fairies. I admit, it was me leaving all those gifts, however, there were times, even when the girls were not staying overnight, that I began to find things around the enchanted cottage—coins mostly, pennies, dimes, and one day even an arrowhead. Now I was excited! This opened up a whole new world for me. While my granddaughters have now grown so much and the world of fae has faded, it has been completely illuminating for me. I have been led to some really fascinating books and documented accounts of fairies and met some amazing people with their own accounts of the fairies. I now have a corner garden that has been transformed into "The Fairy Area." I have enjoyed quiet time there at twilight and seen things that are not explainable, things that can fly so fast you are not really sure what you just saw, or twinkling lights that come and go, and no, they are not fireflies. The knowing in my heart of the existence of this realm is profound."

The following story is my own personal experience with fairies.

"I was in the Chalice Well Garden in Glastonbury, England. It is a fairyland garden with a well and a sparkling little stream running through it—virtually at the base of the famous mount called Glastonbury Tor of King Arthur legend. There are several locations in the garden for silent reflection and meditation, as well as many little corners and crevices for Nature's little beings to live in peace. I was leading an Edgar Cayce tour through the garden, with special focus on the well. And we took time to gather inside a little gazebo-like hut for a group meditation. All of us were on the lookout for fairies and little people. Later, when I was alone and down by the small waterfall and its wonderful song-like sound, I sensed fairies playing among the ions of the tumbling water and flowing stream. I sensed the fairies but could not see them with my carnal eyes, which frustrated me. I decided to close my eyes and see if I could see them with my mind's eye. I could! What had only been flickers of light to my carnal eyes were now many little white-light beings dancing in the mist off the falls. They were bright and bouncy. I smiled with delight at seeing them and was filled with the emotion of thanksgiving. Soon after, I walked a bit further down the stream to where there was pooling water, and sensed more fairies. Again, I could not see them with my carnal eyes, so I closed my eyes and instantly my mind's eye saw them. These were much larger than the white-light fairies near the falls, and these fairies were a bluish-violet color. I was impressed by their size and color. They did not dance like the littler fairies in the fall but appeared to move in a slow, rhythmical motion up and down over the pool and among the surrounding plants."

Message from a Leprechaun

When my youngest brother turned draft age, there was a lottery to see who would get drafted into military service. His number was very low, so it was likely that he'd be drafted soon. This so upset him (the Vietnam War was still raging) that one day on the floor in our parent's home he began praying and crying for a way out or some insight into why this was happening to him. In that moment, he saw a leprechaun! It was standing right next to him. The leprechaun had his hands on his hips and was smiling. He told my brother that there was nothing to be worrying about, because his number, despite how low it was, would never be called. My brother blinked his eyes to be sure he was seeing and hearing this, but in the time it took him to blink, the leprechaun was gone. Even so, my brother got up feeling totally certain that there was nothing to worry about. And as it turned out, his number was never called.

Leprechauns are of the family of elves and are distinctly Irish. Of all my siblings, this younger brother is the most Irish, add to this that my mother is full-blooded Irish, and you see how he might see a leprechaun.

A Scottish Highland Encounter

This next experience was sent to me by a good friend who was a career geologist with a vast knowledge of the influence of gems and stones. Here's his encounter with the fairy world blending into our world.

"My wife and I rented a car and drove to the Scottish Highlands. This would have been in the early 1980s. The experience took place on a ridge near a spectacular waterfall in a state park (National Trust Reserve) called "The Trossachs." We took a nature trail to the waterfall, about a mile or so from the visitor center. The wooded walk was stunningly beautiful with old-growth trees covered in lichen and the ground carpeted in bright green moss. When the sun shined through the trees, it filtered in on slanted rays. The old growth trees were splendid specimens, with really impressive serpentine, gnarled roots at the base of their trunks. Add to this the crystal clear stream gurgling down from the waterfall, and you have a living postcard! We were in the perfect magical forest for an enchanting fairy scape.

"The ridgeline is pure opaque white snow quartz, and I think that the mineralogy amplified the energies there, providing a vibrational field that makes the other dimensional realm much more tangible.

"We found a gorgeous spot in a relatively open grove, and sat on a large fallen tree trunk covered in soft moss. I placed a small quartz crystal on the ground a few feet in front of us, and almost immediately we began to see little starbursts sparkling all around the area! Some were like translucent blue orbs. About a half dozen of the orbs floated near to us. The orb-bubbles transformed into translucent faerie beings, and they seemed to float around the quartz crystal. It was delightful and we could feel their energy. It was delightful. Their energies had a lightness that made us laugh almost as if we were being tickled.

"Then about 100 or so feet away, amidst a darker wooded section, a smoky fog began to swirl about, and move. It captured our attention because of its sudden emergence and interesting gyrations. It then manifested into a tangible, semi-physical form of a being with a human-like body, standing on two hoofed legs, and covered in dark brown hair. The mid-torso was that of a muscular man but it had the head of a bull with short horns. It began to float toward us. The faeries disappeared. This energy startled us and sent shivers up our arms. My wife felt really very scared and wanted to leave. Because it was translucent, I had an intuitive sense of what it was (based somewhat on what I had read in Charles Leadbeater books). I was fascinated. It looked like the gargoyle figures carved on the effacement of some of the local medieval Scottish castles.

"The 'being' began floating closer and closer to us, and then my wife became terrified. In front of the 'gargoyle,' a bright light appeared, and we saw the manifestation of a grandfatherly man with a kind face and short white beard. When he manifested, the gargoyle began to evaporate. The grandfather figure seemed to communicate telepathically with my wife. He told her not to be afraid and that his name was 'Sandy.' My wife immediately felt calmer. He then evaporated.

"Although my wife felt better, she wanted to go back to the car. We walked back to the visitor center.

"I was utterly astonished by what just happened, and it was an event that I wanted to understand more clearly. I meditated on this for a long time, and my eventual conclusions were that the specific area we were in was of extremely high energy and that the quartz content in the area had allowed for a 'full spectrum' aspect of dimensionality. I believe that we were able to see the faeries and the 'gargoyle' because of the unique combination of energies within this concentrated dimensional overlay. I believe that certain forms of 'elementals' are electrical in nature, and that we experienced both the negative electrical life-forms and the positive ones. I originally considered that the 'forms' these beings took was related to our own image of 'good' and 'evil,' and that the grandfather image represented goodness and nurturing while the 'gargoyle' image represented dark forces.

"However, a few years later we saw these 'gargoyle'" figures again! However, they were not quite as big as the one in the Trossachs. We saw one on a rock in the Andes of Venezuela, identical in form, and another one at Stewart Mineral Springs near Mount Shasta, California. I believe that there are 'beings' of the 'elemental' type that are quite conscious, and exist in an electrical format (the fire element), with some on the positive end of the electrical spectrum and some on the negative. The negative beings seem to feed on energy. Both seem to exist more tangibly in high-energy areas. However, the negative ones seem to frequent and exist more within high-energy areas that are somewhat *imbalanced*. I think these are 'plasmic' beings that feed on not only ionic energy, but can feed on emotional energy. My sense is that if you do not react in fear, they are unable to attach."

My friend's use of the term "plasmic" is a reference to the "fourth state of matter," the other three being our familiar solid, liquid, and gaseous states. Plasma is gas that is electrically charged, creating positively or negatively charged particles; and these are called *ions*. As he stated, these encounters occurred in special areas. But knowing this man and his wife, I can tell you that their minds and vibes had much to do with the encounters.

An Encounter at the Edgar Cayce Center

In the early years of my forty–some–year career at the Edgar Cayce organization, I heard this fascinating story about an encounter with colorful brownies inhabiting a large Camellia bush behind the headquarters building on our campus in Virginia Beach, Va. The story goes something like this and would have occurred sometime in the late 1960s:

The elderly leader of the Glad Helpers Prayer Group, Ruth LeNoir, was walking by the large Camellia bush when she saw a community of brownies (the little beings, not the cakes) standing on the leaves. They were dressed in their little red and green outfits with curly–toed shoes, little vests, and elf–like hats. And adding to the magic scene were the beautiful blossoms and enchanting fragrance of the bush itself. Then, the brownies *spoke* to her! They told her to go and get a camera and they would allow her to take a photo of them. She did just that. As she was photographing them, the eldest son of Edgar Cayce, Hugh Lynn Cayce, came out and told Ruth that he could see them from the window of his office. Ruth photographed the brownies with a simple, plastic "box" camera of her time. Once the word got around campus, others came to see the brownies, but none could see them. Puzzled, Ruth and Hugh Lynn decided that the ability to see the brownies had something to do with one's openness to the realms beyond the solid physical world. Now, over 50 years later, those photos have gone missing, and Ruth and Hugh Lynn have passed on to realms beyond this one.

I arrived on campus in 1971, and one of the staff members recounted the story to me, saying that she had indeed seen the photos, and they were amazing—tiny little people standing on the leaves of the Camellia bush.

8

⌘

Demons, Fallen Angels, and the Dark Forces

here is a distinction to be made between fallen angels and demons. The fallen angels are those who rebelled against God and were driven out of heaven. Strictly speaking, demons are destructive *spirits*, and they can *possess* people and animals. In some lore, it is said that they can possess the forces of Nature, as indicated in the statement, "an ill wind blows." Demons were considered to be "unclean spirits." *Spirits* is the key word here. In this case, spirits are not *beings* but *dispositions*, *attitudes*, and *impulses* that inhabit beings. They are demonic *motivations*. And they bring sickness to the healthy, weakness to the strong, foulness to the clean, smuttiness to the upright, and so forth. Cayce's readings teach that there is a very thin line between the sublime and the ridiculous, and demonic spirits often push souls over that line when–despite the best of intentions–they fall into dark thoughts and actions. All demonic spirits are earthbound and temporary, but all angels, even the fallen ones, are immortal. Yet, they are currently restricted from entering the Gates of Heaven. Keep this in mind as we study fallen angels. In the Dead Sea Scrolls of the Essenes, we find these interesting words: "He [God] has created man to govern the world, and has appointed to him two spirits in which to walk until the time of His [God's] visitation: the spirits of truth and injustice. Those born of truth spring from a fountain of light, but those born of injustice spring from a source of darkness. All the children of righteousness are led by the Prince of Light and walk in the ways of light, but all the children of injustice are ruled by the Angel of Darkness and walk in the ways of darkness . . . But the God of Israel and His Angel of Truth will succor all the sons of light. For it is He who created the spirits of Light and Darkness and founded every action upon them and established every deed upon their ways. And He loves the one everlastingly and delights in its works for ever; but the counsel of the other [Darkness] He loathes and for ever hates its ways." (*The Complete Dead Sea Scrolls in English*; Geza Vermes, translator; Penguin Classic Books, 1962)

In what may be a helpful insight, Cayce identifies the "anti-Christ" as a *spirit* rather than a being, a spirit that can possess the best of us and even whole nations! Here's that quote:

Q: In what form does the anti-Christ come, spoken of in Revelation?
A: In the spirit of that opposed to the spirit of truth. The fruits of the spirit of the Christ are love, joy, obedience, long-suffering, brotherly love, kindness. Against such there is no law. The spirit of hate, the anti-Christ, is contention strife, fault-finding, lovers of self, lovers of praise. Those are the anti-Christ, and take possession of groups, masses, and show themselves even in the lives of men.   281-16

And in another helpful reading Cayce stated:

For oft—as may be demonstrated in individualities—there are those who are geniuses and yet are so very close to the border that an emotional shock may make a demon of a genius. There are those activities in which a spiritualized cell, by environment, may make of the demon a saint.   281-63

It is the *spirit* by which a person is *moved in feelings, thoughts, and actions* that affects their condition. And one may shift their spirit with the slightest of shifts in their heart, in their mind—moving from demon to saint or saint to demon.

 I concede the paradox when dealing with the greatest fallen angel, Lucifer (Latin for "light bringer"), who did indeed became Satan, the dark spirit in all demons. But in the deepest mysteries of Lucifer and Satan, this terrible angel can be, and in some lore will be, redeemed and rise again. The Scriptures indicate this, though it is well hidden. Let's briefly explore this.

In legend and Scripture (the name only appears once in Isaiah 14:12), Lucifer carries the surprising epithet of "the Morning Star." Most consider this descriptive name to have been his *prior* to his fall from grace. In Greek, the name may be interpreted as "bringer of the dawn," in other words the bringer of the morning light or morning star. The morning star is Venus, which rises brightly in the morning for 236 days of the year. In Hebrew, the language of the book of Isaiah (circa BC 740–680), the name is *helel*, meaning the "shining one." And the word "morning" comes from the Hebrew word *shahar*, meaning "dawn." As was so often the case in mythologies, cosmic and Nature forces were personified as gods, and Helel and Shahar were ancient deities. One could translate the Hebrew passage in Isaiah, *Helel ben Shahar,* as "O shining one, son of the dawn." In fact, the Latin Vulgate (a Latin edition of the Bible that was primarily translated directly from Hebrew and Greek by St. Jerome and used by the Roman Catholic Church for more than 1,000 years) translates *Helel ben Shahar* as "Lucifer, son of the morning." Here's that passage in Isaiah:

"How art thou fallen from heaven, O Lucifer, son of the morning! How art thou cut down to the ground, which didst weaken the nations! For thou hast said in thine heart: 'I will ascend into heaven, I will exalt my throne above the stars of God: I will sit also upon the mount of the congregation, in the sides of the north: I will ascend above the heights of the clouds; I will be like the most High.' Yet thou shalt be brought down to hell, to the sides of the pit." (Isaiah 14:12-15, KJV)

Only the King James Version of the Bible uses the name Lucifer in this passage. Even the American Standard Version, which is so tightly knit with the King James Version, translates this passage: "O day–star, son of the morning!" The Revised Standard Version retains the sense of a proper noun name by capitalizing the words that replace the Hebrew names *Helel* and *Shahar*, "O Day Star, son of Dawn!"

In Dante's *Inferno* and Milton's *Paradise Lost*, Lucifer is clearly the Morning Star.

Why am I spending so much time on this? Because it is leading us to another passage in Scripture that requires this depth of background.

Confusion arises from a passage in the very last chapter of the Bible, the book of the Revelation 22:16, KJV, in which we find this:

> "I Jesus have sent mine angel to testify unto you these things in the churches. I am the root and the offspring of David, and the bright and morning star."

Now is Jesus "the bright and morning star," or is Lucifer? In the Cayce discourses both are, because Lucifer is redeemed through Jesus, who opened the way for all to repent and return to harmony with the source of life and light. The repentant rebel is a theme found in many sacred stories and teachings. In chapter 20 of the Revelation, Satan is bound and thrown into the bottomless pit, which one might consider to be symbolic of the exorcism of angel Lucifer's rebellious nature and evil urges, freeing him to shine again as the morning star.

In the biblical book of Job, God actually engages Satan (the fallen angel Lucifer) in an assignment:

> "Now there was a day when the sons of God came to present themselves before the Lord, and Satan also came among them. The Lord said to Satan, 'Whence have you come?' Satan answered the Lord, 'From going to and fro on the earth, and from walking up and down on it.' And the Lord said to Satan, 'Have you considered my servant Job, that there is none like him on the earth, a blameless and upright man, who fears God and turns away from evil?' Then Satan answered the Lord, 'Does Job fear God for naught? Hast thou not put a hedge about him and his house and all that

he has, on every side? Thou hast blessed the work of his hands, and his possessions have increased in the land. But put forth thy hand now, and touch all that he has, and he will curse thee to thy face.' And the Lord said to Satan, 'Behold, all that he has is in your power; only upon himself do not put forth your hand.' So Satan went forth from the presence of the Lord." (Job 1:6-12, RSV)

Even after Job passed this terrible test, Satan casts doubt on his faith-fulness and love for God and God's ways, unlike Lucifer/Satan and his angels. Thus, Job is tested even more personally:

"Again there was a day when the sons of God came to present themselves before the Lord, and Satan also came among them to present himself before the Lord. And the Lord said to Satan, 'Whence have you come?' Satan answered the Lord, 'From going to and fro on the earth, and from walking up and down on it.' And the Lord said to Satan, 'Have you considered my servant Job, that there is none like him on the earth, a blameless and upright man, who fears God and turns away from evil? He still holds fast his integrity, although you moved me against him, to destroy him without cause.' Then Satan answered the Lord, 'Skin for skin! All that a man has he will give for his life. But put forth thy hand now, and touch his bone and his flesh, and he will curse thee to thy face.' And the Lord said to Satan, 'Behold, he is in your power; only spare his life.' So Satan went forth from the presence of the Lord, and afflicted Job with loathsome sores from the sole of his foot to the crown of his head." (Job 2:1-7, RSV)

While we're on the subject of fallen angels, let's look at archives of angelology and those listed as the Fallen Angels.

Fallen Angels

At some point in the heavenly activities of the angels, a rebellion occurred. It was led by one of the most beautiful angels, Lucifer, whose Hebrew name means "light bringer," and is associated with the morning or day star, Venus. "How art thou fallen from heaven, O Lucifer, son of the morning!" (Isaiah 14:12, KJV)

According to the Cayce readings, Lucifer, along with many angelic companions, including one named Ariel, "made for the disputing of the influences in the experiences of Adam in the Garden." (262–57) Cayce further explains that the rebellion actually began in the spirit, long before the physical Garden of Eden, with angels fighting against angels. As we read in the biblical Revelation, the rebellious angels were engaged by the archangel Michael and his angelic army, who drove them out of heaven, causing them to fall from their original grace. They were cast into the earth with their leader, Satan, the name given to now fallen Lucifer. (Revelation 12) These are now known as the Angels of Darkness, which include Lucifer (Light Giver), Ariel (once of the Choir of Virtues), Beelzebub (once of the choir of cherubim, whose name means "Lord of the Flies"), Belial (mentioned 178 times in the Cayce readings and is considered by many to be a form of Satan, formerly an angel of the Choir of Virtues), Leviathan (once of the Choir of Seraphim), Procell (once of the Choir of Powers), Raum (once of the Choir of Thrones), Semyaza (formerly of the Choir of Seraphim), Vual (formerly of the Choir of Powers), and Azazel (once of the Order of Cherubim).

During one of his readings, in which he was vulnerable to dark forces, Cayce actually had to struggle to shield himself from the dark angel Azazel. It began when a questioner asked the deeply attuned Cayce to actually contact Azul (one of Azazel's names, which include the variants Azael, Hazazel, and Azrael, meaning "God strengthens"). This dark angel is one of the chiefs of the Fallen Angels. Legend holds that Azazel taught men how to fashion swords and shields, and women how to beautify their eyelids and wear ornaments to entice men to unclean thoughts of sin. He is known as the Rider of the Serpent, Seducer of Men, and Satan's standard bearer. He refused to bow his head before God's newly created Adam—recall that humankind was made lower than the angels but with the potential to judge them. (1 Corinthians 6:3 and Hebrews 2:6–7)

Here is the record of this profound Cayce session. Observe that the archangel Michael, the Guardian of the Way, actually speaks through Cayce as this dangerous moment developed, determined to protect Cayce.

Q: Can you contact Azul for me?

A: Demetrius, Michael, [yes]; Azul, no.

Q: You cannot?

A: Cannot.

Q: Why?

A: There are barriers between this body and Azul, as produced by that between Demetrius and between Michael.

Q: Can you contact Azul for anyone else?

A: Not under these conditions; for I, Michael, speak as the Lord of the Way. Bow thine heads, O ye peoples, that would seek to know the mysteries of that life as makes for those *faltering* steps in men's lives when not applied in the manner as has been laid down. O ye stiff-necked and adulterous generation! Who will approach the Throne that ye may know that there is *none* that surpasses the Son of Man in His approach to *human* experience in the material world!

Q: What is my father's name?

A: No.

Q: Can't you answer that question?

A: To be sure, it may be answered. It will not here.

Q: Why will you not answer these questions, when I want to make sure in order to help?

A: He that seeketh a sign when he standeth in the presence of the Highest authority in the Way may *not* be given a sign, unless he has done in the body that which entitles him to same.

Q: Why is Edgar Cayce surrounded by such wrong vibrations and entities in this great work?

A: For there has been the continued battle with those forces as Michael fought with over the body of Moses. He that leads, or would direct, is continually beset by the forces that would undermine. He that endureth to the end shall wear the Crown. He that aideth in upbuilding shall be entitled to that that he *builds* in his experience. He that faltereth, or would hinder, shall be received in the manner as he hinders.

2897-4

In this next reading, Cayce gives a counter to the influences of evil, clearly identifying the nature of evil in our lives.

Q: Comment on "The devil and Satan, which deceiveth the whole
world, he was sent out into the earth."
A: Did He not—the Christ, the Maker—say this over and over
again? that so long as spite, selfishness, evil desires, evil communications were manifested, they would give the channels through
which that spirit called Satan, devil, Lucifer, Evil One, might work?
Also He has said over and over again that even the devil believes
but trembles. Then he that denies in his life, in his dealings with his
fellow man, that the Spirit of Truth makes free, denies his Lord!
                                                            262-119

During other readings, an angel identified as Halaliel spoke through
Edgar Cayce and was identified among those who fought against the
rebellion.

Q: Who is Halaliel, the one who gave us a message on Oct. 15th?
A: One in and with whose courts Ariel fought when there was the
rebellion in heaven. Now, where is heaven? Where is Ariel, and
who was he? A companion of Lucifer or Satan, and one that made
for the disputing of the influences in the experiences of Adam in
the Garden.   262-57

This angel came through Cayce on several occasions mostly giving
prophecies; see his communications in the chapter on Angels.
   Cayce sought protection from the dark angel, and this was well
warranted. There are many detailed legends recounting the activities
of dark angels. Rabbi Joseph's Midrash of Shemhazai and Azazel (yes,
the very angel Archangel Michael kept from speaking through Cayce)
recounts one of the most detailed insights into angel lore. Here is a
portion of that account:

"When the generation of Enosh [son of Seth, grandson of Adam]
arose and practiced idolatry and when the generation of the Flood
arose and corrupted their actions, the Holy One, Blessed be He,
was grieved that He had created man, as it is said, 'And God repented that he created man, and He was grieved at his heart.'
   "Sometime later, two angels arose, whose names were Shem-

hazai and Azazel, and said before Him: 'O Lord of the universe, did we not say to You when You created Your world, "Do not create man?"' As it is said, 'What is man that You should remember him?' The Holy One, Blessed be He, said to them: 'Then what shall become of the world?' They said before Him. "We will suffice, instead of it.'

"He said, 'It is revealed and well known to me that if perhaps you had lived in that (earthly) world, the evil inclination would have ruled you just as much as it rules over the sons of man, but you would be more stubborn than they.' They said before Him, 'Give us Your sanction and let us descend (and dwell) among the creatures and then You will see how we shall sanctify Your name.' He said to them, 'Descend and dwell among them.'

"Immediately, the Holy One allowed the evil inclination to rule over them, as soon as they descended. When they saw the daughters of man that they were beautiful they began to corrupt themselves with them, as it is said, 'Then the sons of God saw the daughters of man'; they could not restrain their inclination.

"Sometime later, Shemhazai saw a girl whose name was Istehar; fixing his eyes at her he said: 'Listen to my (request).' But she said to him: 'I will not listen to you until you teach me the Name by which you are enabled to ascend to heaven, as soon as You mention it.' He taught her the unspeakable Name.

"What did she do? She mentioned it and by which ascended to heaven. The Holy One said, 'Since she has departed from sin, go and set her among the stars." It is she who shines brightly in the midst of the seven stars of the Pleiades, so that she may always be remembered. Immediately, the Holy One fixed her among the Pleiades [also known as the "Seven Sisters"].

"When Shemhazai and Azazel saw this, they took for them wives, and fathered children. [Genesis 6:1-2: "And it came to pass, when men began to multiply on the face of the ground, and daughters were born unto them, that the sons of God saw the daughters of men that they were fair; and they took them wives of all that they chose."] "Shemhazai begat two children, whose names were Ohya and Hahya. And Azazel was appointed chief over all kinds of dyes and over all kinds of women's ornaments by which they entice men to unclean thoughts of sin.

"Immediately, Metatron sent a messenger to Shemhazai and said to him: 'The Holy One is about to destroy His world, and bring upon it a flood.' Shemhazai stood up and raised his voice and wept aloud, for he was sorely troubled about his sons and (his own) iniquity. And he said: 'How shall my children live, and what shall become of them, for each one of them eats daily a thousand camels, a thousand horses, a thousand oxen, and all kinds (of other animals)?'

"One night the sons of Shemhazai, Ohya and Hahya, saw (visions) in (their) dreams, and both of them saw a dream. One saw a great stone spread over the earth like a table, the whole of which was written over with lines (of writing). And an angel (was seen by him) descending from heaven with a knife in his hand and he was erasing and obliterating all the lines, save one line with four words upon it.

"The other (son) saw a garden, planted whole with (many) kinds of trees and (many) kinds of precious stones. And an angel (was seen by him) descending from heaven with an axe in his hand, and he was cutting down all the trees, so that there remained only one tree containing three branches.

"When they awoke from their sleep they arose in confusion, and, going to their father, they related to him the dreams. He said to them: 'The Holy One is about to bring a flood upon the world, and to destroy it so that there will remain but one man and his three sons.' Upon that, they cried in anguish and wept, saying, 'What shall become of us and how shall our names be perpetuated?' He said to them: 'Do not trouble yourselves, for your names, Ohya and Hahya, will never cease from the mouths of creatures, because every time that men lift (heavy) stones or boats, or anything similar, they will shout and call your names.' With this, their tempers cooled down.

"What did Shemhazai do? He repented and suspended himself between heaven and earth head downwards and feet upwards, because he was not allowed to open his mouth before the Holy One, Blessed be He, and he still hangs between heaven and earth.

"Azazel (however) did not repent. And he is appointed chief

over all kinds of dyes which entice man to commit sin and he still continues to corrupt them."

In the Bible, we find God expressing the fall of the perfect angels:

"You were the signet of perfection, full of wisdom and perfect in beauty. You were in Eden, the garden of God; every precious stone was your covering: sardius, topaz, and diamond, beryl, onyx, and jasper, sapphire, emerald, and carbuncle; and crafted in gold were your settings and your engravings. On the day that you were created they were prepared. With an anointed guardian cherub. I placed you; you were on the holy mountain of God; in the midst of the stones of fire you walked. You were blameless in your ways from the day you were created, until unrighteousness was found in you." (Ezekiel 28:12-15, ESV)

There is redemption for the fallen, as there is for all souls that have become lost in the distractions and temptations of free-willed life and self-centeredness.

Angels of the Dark Side, the "Shells" *(Kellipot)*

Here is the list of the dark angels that came from the dark side with an explanation of their names. These unholy emanations (sefirot) are *shadows* of the Holy Emanations (Sefirot) and come out of the left side of God.

- Thaumiel, the "Twins of God," the "Two-Headed" (doubled-mindedness, wanting both God and mammon).
- Chaigidiel, the "Confusion of God's Power."
- Sathariel, the "Concealment of God," who hides the face of Mercy.
- Camchicoth, "Devourers" or "Wasters."
- Golachab, Golab, and Usiel, the "Destroyers."
- Thagirion, the "Builders of Ugliness."
- Harab Serapel, (considered to be plural) means the "Ravens of Death, the leaders of the infernal regions.
- Samael, "Desolation."

- Gamaliel, "Pollution."
- Lilith, the feminine half of the first Adam, giving Adam 100 children every day, according to Rabbi Eliezer in *The Book of Adam and Eve*.

The Zohar describes Lilith as "a hot fiery female who at first cohabited with man," but when Eve was created, she "flew to the cities of the sea coast," where she is "still trying to ensnare mankind." In Hebrew writings, the name Lilith first appears in the Alphabet of Ben Sira (circa 900s), though images exist of her that date back to Assyria's Golden Age. Many rabbis consider her to have been the temptress of Adam and the mother of Cain.

Lilith is the shadow of none other than Metatron! On the other hand, the *Light* Feminine consciousness associated with the tenth emanation is *Shekhinah*, known as the "Divine Indwelling" and the "Bride of the Lord."

Gnosticism helps us understand this, identifying the female spirit (*he kato Sophia*) who, in her ideal essence, is the "Lightsome Mother" (*he meter he photeine*). In her lower state, however, she is the "Lustful One" (*he prouneikos*), a once virginal goddess who fell from her original purity. Here we can see both her light and shadow sides as well as her ultimate perfection and redemption.

All demons are mortal, but in the Zohar, Lilith is an immortal until the Messianic Day—a day that is prophesied in Isaiah 37:31: "And the remnant that is escaped of the house of Judah shall again take root downward, and bear fruit upward."

Edgar Cayce's readings identify Lilith as the first Eve and the divine half of the Logos incarnate. Cayce states that Lilith, as the fallen and then redeemed Divine Feminine, was perfected through many incarnations, the final one being as Mary, the mother of Jesus, to whom the archangel Gabriel gave this amazing address:

"And having come in, the angel said to her, 'Rejoice, highly favored *one*, the Lord *is* with you; blessed *are* you among women!'

"But when she saw *him*, she was troubled at his saying, and considered what manner of greeting this was. Then the angel said to her, 'Do not be afraid, Mary, for you have found favor with God. And behold, you will conceive in your womb and bring forth a Son, and shall call

His name JESUS. He will be great, and will be called the Son of the Highest; and the Lord God will give Him the throne of His father David. And He will reign over the house of Jacob forever, and of His kingdom there will be no end.'

"Then Mary said to the angel, 'How can this be, since I do not know a man?'

And the angel answered and said to her, '*The* Holy Spirit will come upon you, and the power of the Highest will overshadow you; therefore, also, that Holy One who is to be born will be called the Son of God. Now indeed, Elizabeth your relative has also conceived a son in her old age; and this is now the sixth month for her who was called barren. For with God nothing will be impossible.'" [Luke 1:28-37, NKJV]

Clearly, the angel spoke to this woman as a rare and special soul with a major role to play. This story has all the elements of the Gnostic legend of the Lonesome Mother (Mary) and the Lustful One (Lilith), redeemed in Sophia, the Wise Female.

Redemption and resurrection is a path that all may choose to journey, even Lucifer, as reflected in Scripture. Lucifer, under his moniker "Morning Star," is prophesied to rise again and rejoin the heavenly hosts:

"I am the Alpha and the Omega, the first and the last, the beginning and the end. Blessed are they that wash their robes, that they may have the right to come to the tree of life, and may enter in by the gates into the city." [Revelation 22:13-14, ASV]

And:

"I am the root and the offspring of David, the bright, the morning star. And the Spirit and the bride say, Come. And he that hears, let him say, Come. And he that hearth, let him come. He that will, let him take the water of life freely." [Revelation 22:16-17, ASV]

Seen in these lines are the "root" of David, which was fallen, and the offspring of David, which has risen and become redeemed and restored.

Before we leave this chapter, I feel the need to share Edgar Cayce's concern that we always protect ourselves from dark forces, those within our own emotions and thoughts as well as those potentially around us. He even encouraged us to keep little mantras or affirmations in our hearts and minds as we go throughout our day, thereby staying close to the good, the light, and the constructive thoughts and feelings.

A variation of a protection prayer or affirmation would be: "Open our hearts to those unseen forces that surround the throne of grace, beauty, power, and might, as we wrap about us the protection found in the love for God–consciousness in the thought of the Christ–consciousness." You can modify this however you wish with whatever better reflects your feelings and beliefs. The use of the plural "our" and "we" reflects his teaching that we need to get beyond self, self-centeredness, and selfishness, and to become more aware of the Collective Consciousness of all life, all beings, and how we actually exist in a collective rather than alone in our body. Keeping our shields up with a protective affirmation is a good way to get through each day.

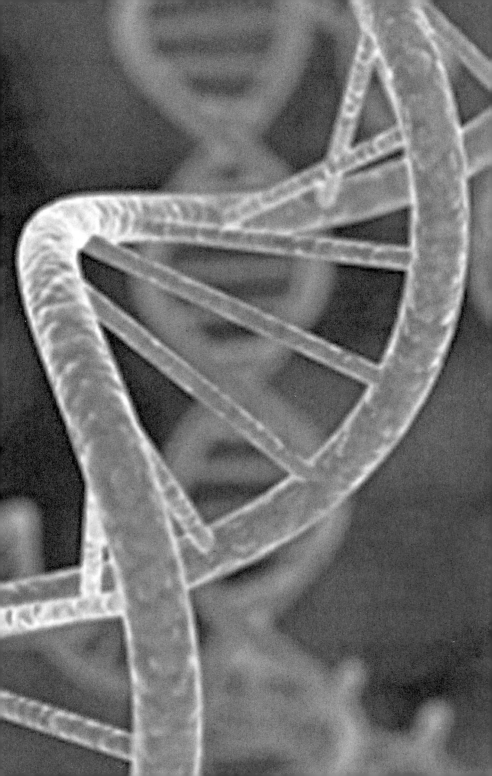

9

⁓◈⁓

The Elementals

Even though many authors include the fairies, sprites, and other little people among the elementals, especially the nature spirits, Edgar Cayce does not. From Cayce's perspective, the elementals are not *beings* but are the fundamental *components* of material life. Using the metaphor of weaving, Cayce identifies the elementals as the "the warp and woof of materiality." (1298-1) The threads in a woven fabric are those that run lengthwise, the *warp*; and those that run crosswise, the *woof* (also called the *weth*). In the case of the elementals, these create the fabric of life. And they are classically known as these four fundamental elements: earth, water, fire, and air. In the Chinese philosophy of *Wu Xing*, they are five in number: wood, earth, water, fire, and gold (literally, the Chinese word here is *gold* but most writers use the English word *metal* instead, don't ask me why!). In the Cayce discourses and ancient Western philosophy, the fifth element is *ether*, from the Latin word meaning "the upper pure, bright air." (440-18, 900-348, 281-27, and 195-70) In India, the fifth element is *Akasha*. The fifth element is considered to be the quintessence of life, as *quint* means "fifth" and *essence* means the intrinsic nature of something without which it would not exist. From this we understand that the elementals are the essential components of life.

The elementals are also considered to be the fundamental forms or states of matter: earth is the solid, water is the liquid, air is the gaseous state, and fire is plasma. The elements of life manifest in any of these forms. In fact, some consider the *fifth* element to actually be plasma rather than fire, relegating fire back to its more common state in this world and associating it with *metabolism*, the combustion necessary to keep a body warm and alive. Plasma is ionized gas or air—meaning the atoms or molecules of a gas are charged. Two examples would be a neon sign, in which the gas inside it is electrically charged, and our Sun, whose gases are supercharged. Plasma, like gas, has no definite shape or definite volume unless enclosed in a container.

Even though they are the essentials of material life and not actual beings, they are considered to be essences from out of which beings emerged. Legend and lore has attributed them to nature spirits in these categories: Gnomes are the spirits of earth, Undines (also called Ondines) are the spirits of water, Salamanders are the spirits of fire, and Sylphs are the spirits of the air (also called Sylphids—depicted as a type of fairy in the ballet *La Sylphide* and Shakespeare's *A Midsummer Night's Dream*). Much of this information was gathered and published by Paracelsus in his alchemical writings of the early 1500s in Europe, and more was published in M.M. Pattison Muir in 1902 in his book, *The Story of Alchemy and the Beginnings of Chemistry*, in Britain. In addition to the four elements, the nature spirits are also personified in three other major life forms: Dryads are the spirits of vegetation, Fauns are the spirits of animal life, and Nymphs are the spirits of the music and dance. There is much more on these "beings" in the chapter on angels.

In many ancient mythologies, the elements are personified as gods of the earth, sea, fire, and wind. In Egypt, the fundamental gods were Geb (earth), Tefnut (water), Path (fire), and Shu (air). We may surmise that Ra, the Sun god, might be the fifth element of plasma; or if we use *ether* as the fifth element, then we might choose Amun-Ra (the invisible god, also written Amon-Ra).

In Greek mythology, they would be: Gaia (earth), Poseidon (sea),

Hephaestus (fire), and Zeus (sky, but also Uranus). While in Roman mythology the gods would be: Tellus or Terra (earth), Neptune (sea), Vulcan (fire), and Jupiter or Jove (sky, but also Caelus).

In an ancient Greek text titled *Kore Kosmou*, meaning "Virgin of the World," and attributed to Hermes Trismegistus, the four elements are explained as the *composition* and *affinity* of various life forms:

"And Isis answered: 'Of living things, my son [her son was Horus], some are made friends with fire, and some with water, some with air, and some with earth, and some with two or three of these, and some with all.

"'And, on the contrary, again some are made enemies of fire, and some of water, some of earth, and some of air, and some of two of them, and some of three, and some of all.

"'For instance, son, the locust and all flies flee fire; the eagle and the hawk and all high-flying birds flee water; fish, air and earth; the snake avoids the open air. Whereas snakes and all creeping things love earth; all swimming things love water; winged things, air, of which they are the citizens; while those that fly still higher love the fire and have the habitat near it. Not that some of the animals as well do not love fire; for instance salamanders, for they even have their homes in it. It is because one or another of the elements doth form their bodies' outer envelope.

"'Each soul, accordingly, while it is in its body is weighted and constricted by these four.'" [Brown, Brian. The Wisdom of the Egyptians, London: Forgotten Books, 2008]

According to the physician Galen of Pergamon (AD 129–216), these four elements were used by the famous physician of the fourth century BC, Hippocrates, the physician who framed the Hippocratic Oath that continues to guide physicians today, and contains the words "do no harm." Hippocrates associated the so-called "four humors" of a human body with the four elements: black bile (earth), phlegm (water), yellow bile (fire), and blood (air). Hippocrates's theory was that the human body contains four basic substances, which he called *humors*. When these are in balance, then a person is healthy. Diseases and disabilities are a result of an excess or deficit of one of these four humors. Even more interesting is how he attributed human temperaments to these elements or humors: Earth (black bile) is despondent, quiet, analytical, and serious; water (phlegm) is calm, thoughtful, patient, and peaceful; fire (yellow bile) is ambitious, leader–like, restless, and easily angered; and air (blood) is courageous, hopeful, playful, and carefree.

When you think of Hippocrates' definitions, keep in mind Isis' teaching that some of us have more than one of these and some may have all four!

Curiously, the Chinese philosophy plays into this idea of balance and imbalance as being health and illness. In the Chinese teaching, the normal life–generating cycle is: wood feeds fire; fire creates earth (ash, or potash in human bodies); earth bears metal; metal collects water; and water nourishes wood. The cycle is in balance. When there is an imbalance, then the corrections are found in these factors: wood parts earth; earth absorbs water; water quenches fire; fire melts metal; metal chops wood. One conclusion from this is how a physician would go about correcting an imbalance by *adding* or *subtracting* elements in the human body to restore balance.

In Hinduism, the five elements are found in the Vedas: earth (*bh mi*), water (*ap* or *jala*), fire (*agni* or *tejas*), air or wind (*marut* or *pavan*), and ether, or "void," or vacuum (*vyom* or *shunya* or *akash*). They correlate the elements to the five senses of hearing, touch, sight, taste, and smell. The lowest element, earth, was created using all of the senses. But water was created using only four of the elements; for it had no odor to smell (we're obviously talking about clean water). Fire can be heard, seen, and felt, so it was created without the use of smell and taste. Air can be heard and felt, thus without the use of smell, taste, and sight. Finally, ether (*Akasha*) is only a medium of sound and is not accessible by the other four senses. The original creation sound according to these teachings was OM, considered to be the *vibration* of the Supreme. OM is sounded in three parts, like ow–uuu–mmm (*ow* as in the sound we make when hurt, "Ow, that hurt."), and represents the divine energy (*Shakti*) united in its three fundamental aspects: creation (*Bhrahma Shakti*), preservation (*Vishnu Shakti*), and liberation through the destruction of illusions (*Shiva Shakti*).

In Buddha's teachings, the four elements are viewed by their *properties*: earth is solidity or inertia, water is cohesion (water molecules stay close to each other), fire is heat and energy, and air is expansion and vibration. Interestingly, Cayce also associates stages of meditation with these properties, as do other mystics: we begin in a solid state (our material bodies) and stillness, then we gradually shift to a more fluid, liquid state as we get deeper into meditation, and then the chakras are awakened and the fire of the Life Force begins to stir, as heated water becomes vapor, we achieve higher vibrations and expand out of our finite condition into a more infinite one and out of our individual consciousness to a more universal consciousness. It may be thought of as moving from ice (solid form), to water (liquid form), and eventually to cloud (vapor).

Today, we have the Periodic Table of the Elements containing 117 elements known in the material world. How have we moved from four elements to this? Because we've moved almost *beyond* the realm of *matter* in our sciences and mathematics! Particle and wave theories, quantum theory, and nanoscopic scales of reality have taken us into the massive space inside matter—in that realm of the Akasha, the void! Remember, all the matter in the universe we see is only four percent of the entire universe. Our understanding is moving closer and closer to the *essence* of life, and it is not just the matter or materiality that the five human senses know.

Where Cayce speaks of the elementals as the "the warp and woof of materiality," he adds, "divinity is the warp and woof of spirituality in the experience of human beings." (1298-1) And from Cayce's mystical view, the elements are not static components of existence but dynamic—attracted and repelled by forces and influences seen and unseen. And we interact with these components of life, as do all life forms—attracting or repelling the elementals of life as we change, as we move through thoughts and actions.

10

❦

Second Sight and the Sixth Sense

n this chapter, I have brought together Edgar Cayce's insights and guidance for developing and improving our perception so that we may perceive angels and the gentler little people, and even sense the elementals of life, both within us and around us. Cayce's English is biblical. And as such it takes some getting used to. But if you read slowly and get comfortable with his sentence structure, he has very helpful information. Words in capital letters reflect a rise in his voice to give emphasis.

Second Sight

We saw Reverend Robert Kirk's use of the term "second sight," and here we see that Edgar Cayce also used the term on occasion.

Curiously, one of the most interesting Cayce discourses on "second sight" came in a reading concerning Atlantis and the natural condition of Atlanteans. Here is that reading as it appears in the Cayce files at the

Association for Research and Enlightenment in Virginia Beach, Va. His stenographer explained that when Edgar would raise the volume of his voice, usually to emphasize a word, she would capitalize the word. The Edgar Cayce Foundation has updated these capitalized words to italics to show emphasis.

TEXT OF READING 364-10
This psychic reading given by Edgar Cayce at his home in Pine-wood on Lake Drive, Virginia Beach, Va., this 28th day of April, 1932, in accordance with request made by those present.

P R E S E N T
Edgar Cayce; Gertrude Cayce, Conductor;
Gladys Davis, Steno. Mildred Davis, H. L. and L. B. Cayce.

R E A D I N G
Time of Reading 3:00 P.M.

GC: You will have before you the information given through this channel on the lost continent of Atlantis. You will please continue with this information, and answer the questions which I will ask regarding same.
EC: Yes. In understanding, then, in the present terminology, occult science, or psychic science—as seen, this was the natural or nature's activity in that experience, and not termed a science—any more than would be the desire for food by a new born babe. Rather the natural consequence. This explanation may of necessity take on some forms that may possibly be confusing at times, but illustrations may be made through the various types of occult science, or psychic manifestations, that may clarify for the student something of the various types of psychic manifestations in the present, as well as that that was natural in this period.

There is, as has been oft given, quite a difference—and much differentiation should be made—in mysticism and psychic, or occult science as termed today.

From that which has been given, it is seen that individuals in the beginning were more of thought forms than individual entities with personalities as seen in the present, and their projections into the realms of fields of thought that pertain to a developing or evolving world of matter, with the varied presentations about same, of the expressions or attributes in the various things about the entity or individual, or body, through which such science—as termed now, or such phenomena as would be termed—became manifest. Hence we find occult or psychic science, as would be called at the present, was rather the natural state of man in the beginning. Very much as (in illustration) when a baby, or babe, is born into the world and its appetite is first satisfied, and it lies sleeping. Of what is its dreams? That it expects to be, or that it has been? Of what are thoughts? That which is to be, or that which has been, or that which is? Now remember we are speaking—these were thought forms, and we are finding again the illustrations of same!

When the mental body (now revert back to what you are calling science)—when the mental body, or mind, has had training, or has gone through a course of operations in certain directions, such individuals are called so-and-so minded; as one of an inventive turn, and trained; one of a statistician turn, and trained; one of a theologian turn, and trained; one of philosophical turn, and trained. Of what does the mind build? We have turned, then, to that that has become very material, for the mind constantly trained makes for itself *mental* pictures, or makes for that as is reasoned with from its own present dimensional viewpoints—but the babe, from whence its reasoning? From whence its dream? From that that has been taken in, or that that has been its experience from whence it came? Oft has it been said, and rightly, with a babe's smile 'Dreaming of angels,' and close in touch with them—but what has *produced* that dream? The contact with that upon which it has fed! Don't forget our premise now from which we are reasoning! And we will find that we will have the premise from which those individuals, or the entities, reasoned within the beginning in this land. (We are speaking of Atlanteans, when they became as thought forces.) From whence did *they* reason? From the Creative Forces from which they had received their impetus, but acted upon by the thought *forms* as were in *material* forms

about them, and given that power (will) to be one *with* that from
what it sprang or was given its impetus, or force, yet with the ability to use that in the way that seemed, or seemeth, good or well, or
pleasing, unto itself. Hence we find in this particular moulding or
mouldive stage, that in which there was the greater development
of, and use of, that as is termed or called psychic and occult forces,
or science—in the present terminology, or age.

Illustrating, then, that as to how this was used by those entities,
those beings, in the formative stage of their experience or sojourn
among that as had been created in all of its splendor to supply
every want or desire that might be called forth by that being, with
all of its attributes physical, mental *and spiritual* at hand; for, as
has been given, even unto the four hundred thousandth generation
from the first creation was it prepared for man's indwelling. As we
today (turn to today), we find there the developments of those
resources. How long have they remained? Since the beginning!
How long has man been able to use them for his undoing, or his
pleasure, or for his regeneration? Since the knowledge of some
source has awakened within its psychic force, or source, of the
apparatus, or the form that it takes, either in a physical or mental
(for remember, Mind is the Builder—and it moves along those
channels through which, and by which, it may bring into existence
in whatever dimension or sphere from which it is reasoning, or
reasoning toward—see)—and as these may be illustrated in the
present:

When there is a manifestation of a psychic force, or an occult
action, or phenomena, or activity in, upon, of or for, an individual,
there is then the rolling back, as it were, or a portion of the physical consciousness—or that mental trained individual consciousness—has been rolled aside, or rolled back, and there is then a
visioning—To what? That as from the beginning, a projection *of*
that form that assumed its position or condition in the earth as
from the beginning, and with those so endowed with that as may
be called an insight into psychic sources there may be visioned
about a body its astral (if chosen to be termed), rather its *thought*
body, as is projected *from* same in such a state; especially so when
there is the induction, or the inducing of, an unconsciousness

of the normal brain, or normal mental body. Submerged—into
what? Into the unconscious, or subconscious. Sub, in *this* instance, meaning *below*—not above normal; below—*subjected* to
the higher consciousness, or to the higher thought, that has been
builded—just as sure as has a physical body been builded, from
what? That as has been given from its first nucleus as passed
through in its experience. Then there may be visioned by such a
body, as may be called with the second sight, or with a vision, that
accompanying thought body of such a one, manifesting in much
the way and manner as individuals in the Atlantean period of psychic and occult development brought about in their experience.
Through such projections there came about that first necessity of
the division of the body, to conform to those necessities of that
as seen in its own mental vision as builded (*mental* now—don't
confuse these terms, or else you will become *very* confused in
what is being given!).

The mental vision by its action upon what body is being builded? On the mental body of the individual in a material world, out of
Spirit, out of the ability to have all the attributes of the spiritual or
unseen forces—but *materialized* forces, as is necessary from the
mental body in a material world *mentally* trained to, or in, certain
directions, or given directions, or following the natural bent of its
threefold or three-ply body, as is seen in every individual or every
entity. As these projected themselves, then we find these *developments* were in this portion of the development in the Atlantean
period. How were these used? In much as were from the beginning. Remember there was ever the instruction to those peoples
that were to hold to that that would bring for the spiritual forces,
rather than the abuses of the abilities—as those with familiar spirits, as those that spoke to or partook of the divinations of those
that had passed from the earth's plane, or those that partook of the
animal magnetism—that came from the universal consciousness
of animal matter as passed into its experience, in its interchange
through those periods of integration and disintegration—and the
spirit forces possessing those that would lay themselves open
to such conditions, for these are as real as physical bodies if the
attunements of the entity are such that it may vision them! And

they are about you always, sure! These, then, are entities—sure; whether animal or those endowed with the soul—until they pass through those changes—as there ever has been, see? Also there are those that ever make for those channels in the psychic and occult (we are speaking of, through which man—as it reached that stage, or that position that it became farther and farther from its natural sources, through the same *character* of channel may it communicate with that from which it is a portion of, or the Creative Forces), and hence the terminology arose as 'Good Spirits' and 'Bad Spirits'; for there are those that partake of the earth, or of the carnal forces, rather than of those forces that are of the spiritual or *creative*. Those that are destruction are of the Earth. Those that are constructive, then, are the good—or the divine and the devilish, bringing for those developments in their various phases. Hence the greater development of that called occult, or psychic forces, during the Atlantean period—and the use of same, and the abuse of same—was during its first thousand years, as we would call light years; not the light of the star, but the sun goes down and the sun goes down—years. That brought about those cycles, or those changes. Hence we have that which has been given through many of the sources of information, or the channels for individuals—and in those, these, the entity—as a voice upon waters, or as the wind that moved among the reeds and harkened, or again as when the morning stars sang together and the sons of God beheld the coming of man into his own, through the various realms as were brought by the magnifying of, or the deteriorating of, the use of those forces and powers as manifested themselves in a *material* area, or those that partook of carnal to the gratification of that that brought about its continual *hardening* and less ability to harken back through that from *which* it came, and partaking more and more *of* that upon which it became an eater of; or, as is seen even in the material forces in the present: We find those that partake of certain elements, unless these become very well balanced *with* all *sources*—of what? That of which there were the first causes, or nature, or natural, or God's sources or forces are. Hence *elements*—not rudiments; elements—as are termed in the terminology of the student of the anatomical, physiological,

psychological forces within a body—germs! Sure they are *germs!*
For each are as atoms of power—from what? That source from
which it has drawn its essence upon what it feeds. Is one feeding,
then, its soul? Or is one feeding its body? Or is one feeding that
inter-between (its mental body) to its own undoing, or to those
foolishnesses of the simple things of life? Being able, then, to partake *of* the physical but not a part of same—but more and more
feeding upon those sources from which it emanates itself, or of
the *spiritual* life, so that the physical body, the mental body, are
attuned *to* its soul forces, or its soul source, its Creator, its Maker,
in such a way and manner, as it develops.

What, then, *is* psychic force? What *is* occult science? A developing of the abilities within each individual that has not lost its
son-ship, or its relation to its Creator, to live upon—or demon-
strate more and more through phenomena of whatever nature
from which it takes its source, for that individual activity of that
entity itself through the stages of development through which it
has passed, and giving of its life source that there may be brought
into being that which gives more knowledge of the source *from*
which the entity essence (isn't a good word, but signifies that intended to be expressed; not elements, not rudiments, but *essence*
of the entity itself, *its* spirit and soul—its spirit being its portion of
the Creator, its soul that of its entity itself, making itself individual,
separate entity, that may be one *with* the Creative Force from
which it comes—or which it is! of which it is made up, in its atomic
forces, or in its very essence itself!) emanates; and the more this
may be manifest, the greater becomes the occult force.

To what uses, then, did these people in this particular period
give their efforts, and in what directions were they active? As
many almost as there were individuals! For, as we find from the records as are made, to some there was given the power to become
the sons of God; others were workers in brass, in iron, in silver,
in gold; others were made in music, and the instruments of music. These, then, we find in the world today. (Today, now—we are
reasoning from today.) Those that are especially gifted in art—in
its various forms; and a real artist (as the world looks at it) isn't
very much fit for anything else! Yet it is—what? An expression of

its concept *of* that from *which* it, that entity, sprang—through the various stages of its evolution (if you choose to call it such) *in* a material world, or that which it fed its soul or its mental being for its development through its varied experiences in a material world. These, then, are but manifestations (occult forces) in individuals who are called geniuses, or gifted in certain directions.

These, then, are the manners in which the *entities*, those *beings*, those *souls*, in the beginning partook of, or developed. Some brought about monstrosities, as those of its (that entity's) association by its projection with its association with beasts of various characters. Hence those of the Styx, satyr, and the like; those of the sea, or mermaid; those of the unicorn, and those of the various forms—these projections of what? The abilities in the *psychic* forces (psychic meaning, then, of the mental *and* the soul—doesn't necessarily mean the body, until it's enabled to be brought *into* being in whatever form it may make its manifestation—which may never be in a material world, or take form in a three-dimensional plane as the earth is; it may remain in a fourth-dimensional—which is an idea! Best definition that ever may be given of fourth-dimension is an idea! Where will it project? Anywhere! Where does it arise from? Who knows! Where will it end? Who can tell! It is all inclusive! It has both length, breadth, height and depth—is without beginning and is without ending! Dependent upon that which it may feed for its sustenance, or it may pass into that much as a thought or an idea. Now this isn't ideal that's said! It's idea! See?)

In the use of these, then, in this material plane—of these forces—brought about those that made for all *manners* of the various forms that are used in the material world today. *Many* of them to a much higher development. As those that sought forms of minerals—and being able to be that the mineral was, hence much more capable—in the psychic or occult force, or power—to classify, or make same in its own classifications. Who classified them? They were from the beginning! They are themselves! They were those necessities as were *in* the beginning from an *all wise* Creator! for remember these came, as did that as was to be the keeper of same! The husbandman of the vineyard! Each entity, each individual—today, has its own vineyard to keep, to dress—for who? Its Maker, from whence it came! What is to be the report in thine own life with those abilities, those forces, as may be manifest in self—through its calling upon, through what? How does prayer reach the throne of mercy or grace, or that from which it emanates? From itself! Through that of *crucifying, nullifying,* the carnal mind and opening the mental in such a manner that the Spirit of truth may flow in its psychic sense, or occult force, into the very being, that you may be one with that from which you came! Be thou faithful unto that committed into thy keeping! Life *itself* is precious! For why? It is of the Maker itself! That *is* the beginning! The psychic forces, the attunements, the developments, going to that! As did many in that experience. And Enoch walked with God, and he was not for God took him. As was many of those in those first years, in this land, this experience.

These in the present, then, do not justly call it science; rather being close to nature. Listen at the birds. Watch the blush of the rose. Listen at the life rising in the tree. These serve their Maker—through what? That psychic force, that *is* Life itself, in their respective sphere—that were put for the service of man. Learn thine lesson, O Man, from that about thee!

We are through for the present.

Here's an excerpt from a past–life reading given for a female nurse who had second sight in a previous incarnation in New England when it was considered to be witchcraft, during that horrible period of history in which "witches" were thought to be doing "Devil's work" and were burned and drowned.

In the one before this we find in this present surrounding, in the present land, under different environs, and during those periods when there were those persecutions in that now known as New England and about that portion of the country now known as Massachusetts. The entity then among those peoples who were misunderstood for the concepts as were gathered *by* those of the entity's group as concerning the activities of unseen forces *in* the material plane. The entity then in the name Marie Jughan, being of those of the group who came westward from the Norwegian land, and of those peoples of that group that were considered as the leaders of this that was not in whole accord with the religious rites [rights] of the period. The entity suffered persecution in the period, but gained through the steadfastness of the understanding as was gained; losing only in the answering back when railed upon by those who would laugh at the entity's physical position, *especially* those days in the stocks as it rained. Hence as is felt in the present, that oft of the daring to do, to be, that as is felt is right, *irrespective* of what others may think, with a *tendency*—sometimes too oft—to give to others that are unappreciative of that *privilege* they are being granted by the knowledge or the manifestation of that being told or shown. In this should the entity, even in the present, take a second thought. As also the experience brings to that is of an intuitive finding, yet oft will the entity find that for *self* the second thought, the second sight, the second determination, is the better. While in many the first impression lasts, to *this* entity *weight* well both sides of *every* question.   2138-1

Here is a Cayce reading for a mother who used her daughter in a previous incarnation to spy on the enemy, and now her psychic daughter returns in this incarnation carrying a fear of the gift and how it may be misused. Cayce clearly indicates that this incarnation is their opportunity to rectify the karma of the previous lifetime:

Q: How have I been associated in the past with the following individuals, what are the urges brought forth in the present, and how may I be of the greatest help to each: First, my daughter [2153]?
A: As we have indicated, there was an association in the sojourn just before this, when there was the using of the daughter's abilities *as* an interpreter or spy into those activities of others. And the developing of the "second sight," as it were, or the psychic abilities, brought fear and doubt; which still exists! and hence may be met in the present.   2344-1

Here's the whole reading for a six-year-old boy whose soul was profoundly involved with the "second sight" for both weal and woe:

TEXT OF READING 4087-1 M 6
This psychic reading given by Edgar Cayce at the office of the
Association, Arctic Crescent, Virginia Beach, Virginia, this 15th
day of April, 1944, in accordance with request made by the fa-
ther—Mr. [...], new Associate Member of the Ass'n for Research
& Enlightenment, Inc., recommended by Mrs. [2455].

P R E S E N T
Edgar Cayce; Gertrude Cayce, Conductor; Gladys Davis, Steno.
(Notes read to and transcribed by Jeanette Fitch.) [4087]'s fa-
ther, Esther Wynne, Mignon Helms, Harmon Bro and others.

R E A D I N G
Born March 24, 1938, Bristol, Rhode Island.
Time of Reading ... Street, 4:05 to 4:25 P. M. Eastern War Time. ...
Rhode Island.

GC: You will give the relations of this entity and the universe, and
the universal forces; giving the conditions which are as personalities, latent and exhibited in the present life; also the former appearances in the earth plane, giving time, place and the name, and
that in each life which built or retarded the development for the
entity; giving the abilities of the present entity, that to which it may
attain, and how. You will answer the questions, as I ask them:
EC: Yes, we have the records here of that entity now known as or
called [4087].

As we find, there are great possibilities but there are also great
problems to be met with the training and the direction for this
entity through the formative years.

For as we find this entity has more than once been among those
who were gifted with what is sometimes called second sight, or
the super-activity of the third eye. Whenever there is the opening,
then, of the lyden (Leydig) center and the kundaline forces from
along the pineal, we find that there are visions of things to come,

of things that are happening.

Yet in the use of these through some experiences, as we will find, the entity is in the present meeting itself. For the entity was the prophet who warned Jereboam. Read it! You will see why he is not to listen at all of those who may counsel him as to the manner in which he is to use the abilities that have been and are a portion of the entity's experience; but to trust in Him who is the way.

Do not get away from the church! In the church keep these activities, that there may be surety in self that has to do or to deal with only the use of such insight, such vision, to the glory of the Father as manifested in the Son.

Do not use such for gratifying, satisfying, or even encouraging the entity to use such. But do train the entity in the use of divine purpose, divine desire. For if the purpose and the desire is right, we may find that the entity may—as in the experience before this—use the activities for the benefit of his fellow man.

For in the use of the power that has been a portion of the entity's consciousness there may come help to many.

For in the experience before this the entity attempted to buy same from Peter. Hence that tendency, that realization that the misuse of same may bring destructive forces into the experience.

In that experience the entity being warned, as he asked "Pray that I may be forgiven for the thought that such might be purchased," he was forgiven. For as it was indicated, "What thou shalt bind on earth shall be bound in heaven, what thou shalt loose on earth shall be loosed in heaven." There we find that the entity through that experience used the ability granted through such for a greater understanding, a greater interpretation. For all of God that any individual may know is already within self. It is in the application and the practice of same within self, in its relations to its desires, its hopes, its fears, and to its fellow man. For as ye sow, ye must reap.

Before that the entity was the prophet of Judah who was sent to Jereboam to warn him, and who brought about the withering of the hand, and also the healing of same; yet turned aside when faced with that in which the mind said "A more excellent way."

There are no short cuts. What God hath commanded is true. For the law of the Lord is perfect and it converteth the soul.

Here the parents have a real, real obligation. They have a real, real opportunity. So live in self that thine own lives may be an example to this entity through its formative years. So teach, not let it be given to someone else—so teach, for it is thy responsibility, not the priest's, not a teacher's, *not* a minister's responsibility, but thine. Don't put it off. Don't neglect, or else ye will meet self again.

In the training let it first begin with self, as with the entity [4087]. Joseph he should be called. Let the training begin with that indicated in Exodus 19:5—"If thou will harken to the voice, He hath a special work, a special mission for thee—but thou must harken to the voice within, that ye present thy body as a living sacrifice, holy and acceptable unto Him, which is a reasonable service." For they who have been called, who have been ordained to be messengers have the greater responsibility; not as a saint—for there is more joy in heaven over one sinner than ninety and nine who are so-called saints, or those who are themselves satisfied with that they do.

Then study that interpreted in Romans. Ye will find it is not from somewhere else, not from out of the blue, not from overseas, not from before the altar. For thy body is indeed the temple and there he may indeed meet his Maker. There indeed may he meet himself. There indeed may he open the door of his own consciousness so that the Master may walk and talk with him.

Do not discourage, do not encourage the visions—until the first lessons are learned.

Then there will be the needs that *thou*, as well as others, take heed to the warnings this entity may be sent to give.

We are through for the present.

Sixth Sense

In the Summer of 1932, Edgar Cayce was asked to do a series of his psychic readings on the "sixth sense" as seen during the sleep state. Here are those three readings exactly as they were transcribed and exist today in the files at the Association for Research and Enlightenment (A.R.E.) in Virginia Beach, Va.:

TEXT OF READING 5754-1
This psychic reading given by Edgar Cayce at his
home on Arctic Crescent, Virginia Beach, Va.,
this 14th day of July, 1932, in accordance with request
made by Hugh Lynn Cayce and those present.

P R E S E N T
Edgar Cayce; Gertrude Cayce, Conductor; Gladys Davis, Steno.
Mildred Davis, Edgar Evans Cayce, and Polly the parrot.
(Also canary in cage)

Time of Reading 4:30 P.M.

GC: You will please outline clearly and comprehensively the material which should be presented to the general public in explaining just what occurs in the conscious, subconscious and spiritual forces of an entity while in the state known as sleep. Please answer the questions which will be asked regarding this:

EC: Yes. While there has been a great deal written and spoken regarding experiences of individuals in that state called sleep, there has only recently been the attempt to control or form any definite idea of what produces conditions in the unconscious, subconscious, or subliminal or subnormal mind, by attempts to produce a character—or to determine that which produces the character—of dream as had by an individual or entity. Such experiments may determine for some minds questions respecting the claim of some psychiatrist or psycho-analyst and through such experiments refute or determine the value of such in the study of certain character of mental disturbances in individuals; yet little of this may be called true analysis of what happens to the body, either physical, mental, subconscious or spiritual, when it loses itself in such repose. To be sure, there are certain definite conditions that take place respecting the physical, the conscious, and the subconscious, as well as spiritual forces of a body.

So, in analyzing such a state for a comprehensive understanding, all things pertaining to these various factors must be considered.

First, we would say, sleep is a shadow of, that intermission in earth's experiences of, that state called death; for the physical consciousness becomes unaware of existent conditions, save as are determined by the attributes of the physical that partake of the attributes of the imaginative or the subconscious and unconscious forces of that same body; that is, in a normal sleep (physical stand-point we are reasoning now) the *senses* are on guard, as it were, so that the auditory forces are those that are the more sensitive.

The auditory sense being of the attributes or senses that are more universal in aspect, when matter in its evolution has become aware of itself being capable of taking from that about itself to sustain itself in its present state. That is as of the lowest to the highest of animate objects or beings. From the lowest of evolution to the highest, or to man.

So, then, we find that there are left what is ordinarily known as four other attributes that are acting independently and coordinat-ingly in *awareness* for a physical body to be conscious. These, in the state of sleep or repose, or rest, or exhaustion, or induced by any influence from the outside, have become *unaware* of that which is taking place about the object so resting.

Then, there is the effect that is had upon the body as to what becomes, then, more aware to those attributes of the body that are not aware of that existent about them, or it. The organs that are of that portion known as the inactive, or not necessary for conscious movement, keep right on with their functioning—as the pulsations, the heartbeat, the assimilating and excretory system, keep right on functioning; yet there are periods during such a rest when even the heart, the circulation, may be said to be at rest. What, then, *is* that that is not in action during such period? That known as the sense of perception as related to the physical brain. Hence it may be truly said, by the analogy of that given, that the auditory sense is sub-divided, and there is the act of hearing by feeling, the act of hearing by the sense of smell, the act of hearing by *all* the senses that are independent of the brain centers them-selves, but are rather of the lymph centers—or throughout the entire sympathetic system is such an accord as to be *more* aware, *more* acute, even though the body-physical and brain-physical is at repose, or *unaware.*

Of what, then, does this sixth sense partake, that has to do so much with the entity's activities by those actions that may be brought about by that passing within the sense *range* of an entity when in repose, that may be called—in their various consider-ations or phases—experiences of *something* within that entity, as a dream—that may be either in toto to that which is to happen, is happening, or may be only presented in some form that is emblem-atical—to the body or those that would interpret such.

These, then—or this, then—the sixth sense, as it may be termed for consideration here, partakes of the *accompanying* entity that is ever on guard before the throne of the Creator itself, and is that that may be trained or submerged, or left to its *own* initiative until it makes either war *with* the self in some manner of expres-sion—which must show itself in a material world as in dis-ease, or disease, or temper, or that we call the blues, or the grouches, or any form that may receive either in the waking state or in the sleep state, that has *enabled* the brain in its activity to become so changed or altered as to respond much in the manner as does a string tuned that vibrates to certain sound in the manner in which it is strung or played upon.

Then we find, this sense that governs such is that as may be known as the other self of the entity, or individual. Hence we find there must be some definite line that may be taken by that other self, and much that then has been accorded—or recorded—as to that which may produce certain given effects in the minds or bod-ies (not the minds, to be sure, for its active forces are upon that outside of that in which the mind, as ordinarily known, or the brain centers themselves, functions), but—as may be seen by all such experimentation, these may be produced—the same effect—upon the same individual, but they do not produce the same effect upon a different individual in the same environment or under the same circumstance. Then, this should lead one to know, to understand, that there is a *definite* connection between that we have chosen to term the sixth sense, or acting through the auditory forces of the body-physical, and the other self within self.

In purely physical, we find in sleep the body is *relaxed*—and there is little or no tautness within same, and those activities that function through the organs that are under the supervision of the sub-conscious or unconscious self, through the involuntary activities of an organism that has been set in motion by that impulse it has received from its first germ cell force, and its activity by the union *of* those forces that have been impelled or acted upon by that it has fed upon in all its efforts and activities that come, then it may be seen that these may be shown by due consideration—that the same body fed upon *meats*, and for a period—then the same body fed upon only herbs and fruits—would *not* have the same character or activity of the other self in its relationship to that as would be experienced by the other self in its activity through that called the dream self.

We are through for the moment—present.

TEXT OF READING 5754-2
This psychic reading given by Edgar Cayce at his home on Arctic Crescent, Virginia Beach, Va., this 15th day of July, 1932, in accordance with request made by those present.

P R E S E N T
Edgar Cayce; Gertrude Cayce, Conductor;
Gladys Davis, Steno. Mildred Davis.

R E A D I N G
Time of Reading 11:30 A.M.

EC: Now, with that as has just been given, that there is an active force within each individual that functions in the manner of a sense when the body-physical is in sleep, repose or rest, we would then outline as to what are the functions of this we have chosen to call a sixth sense.

What relation does it bear with the normal physical recognized five senses of a physical-aware body? If these are active, what relation do they bear to this sixth sense?

Many words have been used in attempting to describe what the spiritual entity of a body is, and what relations this spirit or soul bears with or to the active forces within a physical normal body. Some have chosen to call this the cosmic body, and the cosmic body as a sense in the universal consciousness, or that portion of same that is a part of, or that body with which the individual, or man, is clothed in his advent into the material plane.

These are correct in many respects, yet by their very classification, or by calling them by names to designate their faculties or functionings, have been limited in many respects.

But what relation has this sixth sense (as has been termed in this presented) with this *soul* body, this cosmic consciousness? What relation has it with the faculties and functionings of the normal physical mind? Which must be trained? The sixth sense? Or must the body be trained in its other functionings to the dictates of the sixth sense?

In that as presented, we find this has been termed, that this ability or this functioning—that is so active when physical consciousness is laid aside—or, as has been termed by some poet, when the body rests in the arms of Morpheus—is nearer possibly to that as may be understandable by or to many; for, as given, this activity—as is seen—of a mind, or an attribute of the mind in physical activity—*leaves* a *definite* impression. Upon what? The mental activities of the body, or upon the subconscious portion of the body (which, it has been termed that, it never forgets), upon the spiritual essence of the body, or upon the soul itself? These are questions, not statements!

In understanding, then, let's present illustrations as a pattern, that there may be comprehension of that which is being presented:

The activity, or this sixth sense activity, is the activating power or force of the other self. What other self? That which has been builded by the entity or body, or soul, through its experiences as a whole in the material and cosmic world, see? Or is as a faculty of the soul-body itself. Hence, as the illustration given, does the subconscious make aware to this active force when the body is at rest, or this sixth sense, some action on the part of self or another that is in disagreement with that which has been builded by that other self, then *this* is the warring of conditions or emotions within an individual. Hence we may find that an individual may from sorrow *sleep* and wake with a feeling of elation. What has taken place? We possibly may then understand what we are speaking of. There has been, and ever when the physical consciousness is at rest, the other self communes with the *soul* of the body, see? Or it goes *out* into that realm of experience in the relationships of all experiences of that entity that may have been throughout the *eons* of time, or in correlating *with* that as it, that entity, *has* accepted as its criterion or standard of judgments, or justice, within its sphere of activity.

Hence through such an association in sleep there may have come that peace, that understanding, that is accorded by that which has been correlated through that passage of the selves of a body in sleep. Hence we find the more spiritual-minded individuals are the more easily pacified, at peace, harmony, in normal active state as well as in sleep. Why? They have set before themselves (now we are speaking of one individual!) that that is a criterion that may be wholly relied upon, for that from which an entity or soul sprang is its *concept*, its awareness of, the divine or creative forces within their experience. Hence they that have named the Name of the Son have put their trust in Him. He is their standard, their model, their hope, their activity. Hence we see how that the action through such sleep, or such quieting as to enter the silence—what do we mean by entering the silence? Entering the presence of that which *is* the criterion of the selves of an entity!

On the other hand oft we find one may retire with a feeling of elation, or peace, and awaken with a feeling of depression, of aloofness, of being alone, of being without hope, or of fear entering, and the *body-physical* awakes with that depression that manifests itself as of low spirits, as is termed, or of coldness, gooseflesh over the body, in expressions of the forces. What has taken place? A comparison in that "arms of Morpheus," in that silence, in that relationship of the physical self being unawares of those comparisons between the soul and its experiences of that period with the experiences of itself throughout the ages, and the experience may not have been remembered as a dream—but it lives *on*—and on, and must find its expression in the relationships of all it has experienced in whatever sphere of activity it may have found itself. Hence we find oft individual circumstances of where a spiritual-minded individual in the material plane (that is, to outward appearances of individuals so viewing same) suffering oft under pain, sickness, sorrow, and the like. What takes place? The experiences of the soul are meeting that which it has merited, for the clarification for the associations of itself with that whatever has been set as its ideal. If one has set self in array against that of love as manifested by the Creator, in its activity brought into material plane, then there *must* be a continual—continual—*warring* of those elements. By the comparison we may find, then, how it was that, that energy of creation manifested in the Son—by the activities of the Son in the material plane, could say "He sleeps," while to the outward eye it was death; for He was—and is—and ever will be—Life and Death in one; for as we find ourselves *in* His presence, that we have builded in the soul makes for that condemnation or that pleasing of the presence of that in His presence. So, my son, let thine lights be in Him, for these are the *manners* through which all may come to an understanding of the activities; for, as was given, "I was in the Spirit on the Lord's day." "I was caught up to the seventh heaven. Whether I was in the body or out of the body I cannot tell." What was taking place? The subjugation of the physical attributes in accord and attune with its infinite force as set as its ideal brought to that soul, "Well done, thou good and faithful servant, enter into the joys of thy Lord." "He that would be the greatest among you—" Not as the Gentiles, not as the heathen, not as the scribes or Pharisees, but "He that would be the greatest will be the *servant* of all."

What, then, has this to do—you ask—with the subject of sleep? Sleep—that period when the soul takes stock of that it has acted upon during one rest period to another, making or drawing—as it were—the comparisons that make for Life itself in its *essence*, as for harmony, peace, joy, love, long-suffering, patience, brotherly love, kindness—these are the fruits of the Spirit. Hate, harsh words, unkind thoughts, oppressions and the like, these are the fruits of the evil forces, or Satan and the soul either abhors that it has passed, or enters into the joy of its Lord. Hence we see the activities of same. This an *essence* of that which is intuitive in the active forces. Why should this be so in one portion, or one part of a body, rather than another? How received woman her awareness? Through the sleep of the man! Hence *intuition* is an attribute of that made aware through the suppression of those forces from that from which it sprang, yet endowed *with* all of those abilities and forces of its Maker that made for same its activity in an *aware* world, or—if we choose to term it such—a three dimensional world, a *material* world, where its beings must see a materialization to become aware of its existence in that plane; yet all are aware that the essence of Life itself as the air that is breathed—carries those elements that are not aware consciously of any existence to the body, yet the body subsists, lives upon such. In sleep all things become possible, as one finds self flying through space, lifting, or being chased, or what not, by those very things that make for a comparison of that which has been builded by the very soul of the body itself.

What, then, is the sixth sense? Not the soul, not the conscious mind, not the subconscious mind, not intuition alone, not any of those cosmic forces—but the very force or activity of the soul in its experience through *whatever* has been the experience of that soul itself. See? The same as we would say, is the mind of the body the body? No! Is the sixth sense, then, the soul? No! No more than the mind is the body! For the soul is the *body* of, or the spiritual essence of, an entity manifested in this material plane.

We are through for the present.

TEXT OF READING 5754-3
This psychic reading given by Edgar Cayce at his
home on Arctic Crescent, Va. Beach, Va. this 15th day of July,
1932, in accordance with request made by those present.

PRESENT
Edgar Cayce; Gertrude Cayce, Conductor;
Gladys Davis, Steno. Mildred Davis.

READING
Time of Reading 4:45 P.M.

EC: Yes, we have that which has been given here. Now, as we have that condition that exists with the body and this functioning, or this sense, or this ability of sleep and sense, or a sixth sense, just what, how, may this knowledge be used to advantage for an individual's development towards that it would attain?

As to how it may be used, then, depends upon what is the ideal of that individual; for, as has been so well pointed out in Holy Writ, if the ideal of the individual is lost, then the abilities for that faculty or that sense of an individual to contact the spiritual forces are gradually lost, or barriers are builded that prevent this from being a sensing of the nearness of an individual to a spiritual development.

As to those who are nearer the spiritual realm, their visions, dreams, and the like, are more often—and are more often retained by the individual; for, as is seen as a first law, it is self-preservation. Then self rarely desires to condemn self, save when the selves are warring one with another, as are the elements within a body when eating of that which produces what is termed a nightmare—they are warring with the senses of the body, and partake either of those things that make afraid, or produce visions of the nature as partaking of the elements that are taken within the system, and active within same itself. These may be given as examples of what it is all about.

Then, how may this be used to develop a body in its relationship to the material, the mental, and the spiritual forces?

Whether the body desires or not, in sleep the consciousness physically is laid aside. As to what will be that it will seek, depends upon what has been builded as that it would associate itself with, physically, mentally, spiritually, and the closer the association in the mental mind in the physical forces, in the physical attributes, are with spiritual elements, then—as has been seen by even those attempting to produce a certain character of vision or dream—these follow much in that; for another law that is universal becomes active! Like begets like! That which is sown in honor is reaped in glory. That which is sown in corruption cannot be reaped in glory; and the likings are associations that are the companions of that which has been builded; for such experiences as dreams, visions and the like, are but the *activities* in the unseen world of the real self of an entity.

Ready for questions.

(Q) How may one train the sixth sense?

(A) This has just been given; that which is constantly associated in the mental visioning in the imaginative forces, that which is constantly associated with the senses of the body, that will it develop toward. What is that which is and may be sought? When under stress many an individual—there are *no* individuals who haven't at *some time* been warned as respecting that that may arise in their daily or physical experience! Have they heeded? Do they heed to that as may be given as advice? No! It must be experienced!

(Q) How may one be constantly guided by the accompanying entity on guard at the Throne?

(A) It is there! It's as to whether they desire or not! It doesn't leave but is the active force. As to its ability to sense the variations in the experiences that are seen, is as has been given in the illustration—"As to whether in the body or out of the body, I cannot tell." Hence this sense is that ability of the entity to associate its physical, mental or spiritual self to that realm that it, the entity, or the mind of the soul, seeks for its association during such periods—see? This might confuse some, for—as has been given—the subconscious and the abnormal, or the unconscious conscious, is the mind of the soul; that is, the sense that this is used, as being that subconscious or subliminal self that is on guard ever with the Throne itself; for has it not been said, "He has given his angels charge concerning thee, lest at any time thou dashest thy foot against a stone?" Have you heeded? Then He is near. Have you disregarded? He has withdrawn to thine own self, see? That self that has been builded, that that is as the companion, that must be presented—that *is* presented—*is* before the Throne itself! *Consciousness*—[physical] consciousness—see—man seeks this for his own diversion. In the sleep [the soul] seeks the *real* diversion, or the *real* activity of self.

(Q) What governs the experiences of the astral body while in the fourth dimensional plane during sleep?

(A) This is, as has been given, that upon which it has fed. That which it has builded; that which it seeks; that which the mental mind, the subconscious mind, the subliminal mind, *seeks*! That governs. Then we come to an understanding of that, "He that would find must seek." In the physical or material this we understand. That is a pattern of the subliminal or the spiritual self.

(Q) What state or trend of development is indicated if an individual does not remember dreams?

(A) The negligence of its associations, both physical, mental and spiritual. Indicates a very negligible personage!

(Q) Does one dream continually but simply fail to remember consciously?

(A) Continues an association or withdraws from that which is its right, or its ability to associate! There is no difference in the unseen world to that that is visible, save in the unseen so much greater expanse or space may be covered! Does one always desire to associate itself with others? Do individuals always seek companionship in this or that period of their experiences in each day? Do they withdraw themselves from? That desire lies or carries on! See? It's a *natural* experience! It's not an unnatural! Don't seek for unnatural or supernatural! It is the natural—it is nature—it is God's activity! His associations with man. His *desire* to make for man a way for an understanding! Is there seen or understood fully that illustration that was given of the Son of man, that while those in the ship were afraid because of the elements the Master of the sea, of the elements, slept? What associations may there have been with that sleep? Was it a natural withdrawing? Yet when spoken to, the sea and the winds obeyed His voice. Thou may do even as He, wilt thou make thine self aware—whether that awareness through the ability of those forces within self to communicate with, understand, those elements of the spiritual life *in* the conscious and unconscious, these be one!

(Q) Is it possible for a conscious mind to dream while the astral or spirit body is absent?

(A) There may be dreams. (This is a division here.) A conscious mind, while the body is absent, is as one's ability to divide self and do two things at once, as is seen by the activities of the mental mind.

The ability to read music and play is using different faculties of the same mind. Different portions of the same consciousness. Then, for one faculty to function while another is functioning in a different direction is not only possible but probable, dependent upon the ability of the individual to concentrate, or to centralize in their various places those functionings that are manifest of the spiritual forces in the material plane. *Beautiful*, isn't it?

(Q) What connection is there between the physical or conscious mind and the spiritual body during sleep or during an astral experience?

(A) It's as has been given, that *sensing*! With what? That separate sense, or the ability of sleep, that makes for acuteness with those forces in the physical being that are manifest in everything animate. As the unfolding of the rose, the quickening in the womb, of the grain as it buds forth, the awakening in all nature of that which has been set by the divine forces, to make the awareness of its presence in *matter*, or material things.

We are through for the present.

According to Cayce's lessons, *knowing* how something may be developed is quite different from *applying* that knowledge in daily life, and gaining experience with each application. Cayce taught that it is in the *doing* that the understanding comes. If we want a broader perception of reality, then we must practice such perception in little ways each day, step by step, here a little and there a little, until it becomes our natural awareness.

Who Was Edgar Cayce?
Twentieth Century Psychic and Medical Clairvoyant

Edgar Cayce (pronounced Kay-Cee, 1877-1945) has been called the "sleeping prophet," the "father of holistic medicine," and the most-documented psychic of the 20th century. For more than 40 years of his adult life, Cayce gave psychic "readings" to thousands of seekers while in an unconscious state, diagnosing illnesses and revealing lives lived in the past and prophecies yet to come. But who, exactly, was Edgar Cayce?

Cayce was born on a farm in Hopkinsville, Kentucky, in 1877, and his psychic abilities began to appear as early as his childhood. He was able to see and talk to his late grandfather's spirit, and often played with "imaginary friends" whom he said were spirits on the other side. He also displayed an uncanny ability to memorize the pages of a book simply by sleeping on it. These gifts labeled the young Cayce as strange, but all Cayce really wanted was to help others, especially children.

Later in life, Cayce would find that he had the ability to put himself into a sleep-like state by lying down on a couch, closing his eyes, and folding his hands over his stomach. In this state of relaxation and meditation, he was able to place his mind in contact with all time and space—the universal consciousness, also known as the super-conscious mind. From there, he could respond to questions as broad as, "What are the secrets of the universe?" and "What is my purpose in life?" to as specific as, "What can I do to help my arthritis?" and "How were the pyramids of Egypt built?" His responses to these questions came to be called "readings," and their insights offer practical help and advice to individuals even today.

The majority of Edgar Cayce's readings deal with holistic health and the treatment of illness. Yet, although best known for this material, the sleeping Cayce did not seem to be limited to concerns about the physical body. In fact, in their entirety, the readings discuss an astonishing 10,000 different topics. This vast array of subject matter can be narrowed down into a smaller group of topics that, when compiled together, deal with the following five categories: (1) Health-Related Information; (2) Philosophy and Reincarnation; (3) Dreams and Dream Interpretation; (4) ESP and Psychic Phenomena; and (5) Spiritual Growth, Meditation, and Prayer.

Learn more at EdgarCayce.org.

What Is A.R.E.?

Edgar Cayce founded the non-profit Association for Research and Enlightenment (A.R.E.) in 1931, to explore spirituality, holistic health, intuition, dream interpretation, psychic development, reincarnation, and ancient mysteries—all subjects that frequently came up in the more than 14,000 documented psychic readings given by Cayce.

The Mission of the A.R.E. is to help people transform their lives for the better, through research, education, and application of core concepts found in the Edgar Cayce readings and kindred materials that seek to manifest the love of God and all people and promote the purposefulness of life, the oneness of God, the spiritual nature of humankind, and the connection of body, mind, and spirit.

With an international headquarters in Virginia Beach, Va., a regional headquarters in Houston, regional representatives throughout the U.S., Edgar Cayce Centers in more than thirty countries, and individual members in more than seventy countries, the A.R.E. community is a global network of individuals.

A.R.E. conferences, international tours, camps for children and adults, regional activities, and study groups allow like-minded people to gather for educational and fellowship opportunities worldwide.

A.R.E. offers membership benefits and services that include a quarterly body-mind-spirit member magazine, Venture Inward, a member newsletter covering the major topics of the readings, and access to the entire set of readings in an exclusive online database.

Learn more at EdgarCayce.org.

EDGARCAYCE.ORG